CONTENTS

INTRODUCTION

Are you seeking a healthy physique and enticing figure? Or have you been considering starting a weight loss program for ages but have yet not taken that bold step to achieving goal? The Internet is full of prescriptions for people who want to lose weight, but not everything you read online will work for you. weight is more effectively controlled when you watch what you eat. This is where the ketogenic diet comes in. The keto scheme affords you the opportunity to effortlessly burn fat. If you follow this diet, weight loss will be the reward for dedication. And there are more benefits to enjoy, like engaging in activities that carrying excess weight has prevented you from partaking in. Also, the freedom and self-love that the keto diet offers is one-of-a-kind. You'll be enriched with more energy as you get into this program.

Mental sharpness and quick thinking are among the numerous benefits of a ketogenic diet. Debilitating medical conditions such as cardiovascular disease, abnormal blood sugar levels, and distorted cholesterol levels are often better managed when you are on a keto diet. This goes a long way to increase the quality of life. In fact, the ancient Greeks used this type of diet to cure epilepsy.

Our primary aim is to provide you with some of the most delicious and healthy recipes to help diet run effectively. For both keto diet beginners and those who have been using keto for a long time now, the recipes contained in this book are extremely delicious. They are so fast and easy to prepare that they ensure that you do not spend all of precious time in the kitchen. They are written with precision. Each recipe write up features the ingredients, instructions, preparation time, cooking time, and number of servings, as well as the nutritional value.

The fact that you decided to buy this book shows that you are serious about embarking on a ketogenic diet. It is also possible that you are already a keto diet fan who is looking for an exhaustive guide with more recipes. If so, then this book if for you. Regardless of the main reason for reading this book, it will expose you to the ideal culinary methods for the ketogenic diet.

DESSERTS AND THE KETO DIET PHILOSOPHY

Of course, the term "dessert" needs no introduction for most people. But for the purpose of this book, desserts are generally a small meal that is eaten after a major meal. Usually they consist of sweet foods, like confections, fruits, or beverages like dessert liqueur or wine. However, in the US, desserts can also include cheeses, nuts, coffee, and other sweet foods that are regarded as independent meals elsewhere. Some other countries do not have desserts in their dietary regimen.

The ketogenic diet, also called the keto diet, is certainly not a recently developed dieting scheme. It has been around since ancient times, when Greeks first used the dieting scheme as a treatment for epileptic patients. Even here in the United States, it was a recognized method for treatment of people with epileptic seizures in the 1920s. Unfortunately, this natural way of using food as medicine was sacrificed in favor of cutting-edge pharmaceutical science with its more immediate effects. Thankfully, the ketogenic diet has found its way back into the modern world once more! The premise of the ketogenic diet is to trigger body's fat consumption systems to fuel what the body requires for vitality throughout the day. This means the fat that you eat, as well as the stored fat in body, become fuel stores that body can tap! Little wonder that this dieting routine truly causes weight reduction for those who regularly engage in it. This could be one of the reasons why you picked up this book in the first place. There are also accounts of type 2 diabetes being defeated simply by using this diet. Some statistics suggest that engaging in the keto diet can even cure some malignant growths. Even though the dieting scheme offers untold benefits, there are also some disadvantages related to keto diets. We recommend that you speak to doctor before embarking on this diet.

BENEFITS OF THE KETOGENIC DIET

Helps suppress hunger

Engaging in the keto diet naturally suppresses hunger. This is most important when you are using the diet for weight loss. It prevents those annoying hunger pangs. The manner in which weight is lost is gradual rather than sudden. While engaging in this kind of diet, you'll not be forced to watch out for those dreaded weight gains that come when you resume normal eating style after starving self to lose weight. This is because there is a sequence of reactions that occur in the human body called ketosis, and this reaction doesn't permit weight gain. Of course, if you eat excessively, you'll until gain weight. Because of the immense benefit these kinds of food confer to nervous system, they'll go a long way to give you a clearer and sharper mind. This is in contrast to the usual brain fog experienced by people who eat carbohydrate-rich foods. Ketones, the category that ketogenic foods belong to, are more efficient food sources. They have also been associated with improved brain function. When the human body is in ketosis, the body switches its energy sources to ketones which help to generate energy. These ketones also serve as materials used by the body to make certain brain chemicals such as glutamate and gamma amino butyric acid (GABA). These brain chemicals are called neurotransmitters and they play a huge role in the transmission of information throughout our brain. GABA, for example, is the brain chemical that has been implicated in helping the brain to calm down. Glutamate, on the other hand, serves as a stimulant for the brain. The intrinsic demand to be happy and healthy ensures that these chemicals remain in a dynamic balance, in the right proportion that is required in the brain.

Increases energy level

Rather than experiencing unstable energy levels caused by eating some kinds of food, the ketogenic diet offers increased energy levels in body for a longer period of time. Chronic fatigue becomes a thing of the past, regardless of its source. Whether the fatigue is as a result of a disease or overworking, the ketogenic diet serves to increase energy levels. With the consumption of the appropriate amount of omega-3 fatty acids, you'll become less susceptible to inflammation. This is quite helpful when you are suffering from a chronic disease. Because you'll be on a low-carbohydrate diet, inflammation will be significantly reduced. Reduced intake of carbohydrates means that the blood level of triacylglycerides would be also reduced because they are biosynthesized by carbohydrates. Triacylglycerols are produced with the additional calories provided by carbohydrates. When ketones become the body's predominant fuel, there is a decreased need for triacylglycerides production. When you are on a keto diet, desire to eat springs from actual hunger and not from the frequent instability of blood sugar levels.

Increases the level of "good fats" in body

When you get on a keto diet, the level of good lipids (HDL) increases while the level of bad lipids (LDL) levels decrease. There are certain cases in which the levels of good and bad lipids both increase so that the overall levels of lipids in system rises.

Decreases insulin levels and blood sugar

Ketogenic diets can be especially useful for individuals with diabetes and insulin obstruction. Studies show that cutting down on carbs in our diets brings both glucose and insulin levels down radically. Some people with diabetes who start a low-carb diet may soon be able to decrease their insulin supplements by half.

In one examination in individuals with type 2 diabetes, 95% had reduced or eliminated their glucose-lowering medicine within six months. If you take glucose supplements, talk with a doctor before making changes to carb consumption. Engaging in the keto diet when you are on glucose supplement can lead to an undesirable effect such as hypoglycemia.

Decreases blood pressure

Elevated blood pressure, or hypertension, is a major factor for disease, including stroke, kidney failure, and coronary disease.

Eating low-carb foods is a compelling way to lower blood pressure, which ought to lessen the danger of these illnesses and enable you to live longer.

Effectively controls metabolic syndrome

Metabolic disorder is a condition connected with diabetes and coronary illness. Truth be told, metabolic disorder includes:

- Elevated blood pressure
- Abdominal obesity
- Elevated fasting blood sugar levels
- High triglycerides

BARS

01. No-Bake Chocolate "Oatmeal" Bars

Preparation time: 15 minutes
Cook time: 10 minutes
Servings: 16

Ingredients:

Crust Ingredients:

- 1 cup of chopped almonds
- 1 cup of unsweetened coconut flakes
- ½ cup of granulated Erythritol-based Sweetener
- 1 tsp. of yacón Syrup (optional)
- 1 stick (½ cup) of unsalted butter
- ¼ tsp. of salt
- 100g (1 cup) blanched almond flour
- ½ tsp. of Vanilla extract

Filling Ingredients:

- 1¼ cups of heavy Whipping Cream
- 4 oz. finely chopped unsweetened chocolate
- 2 tbsp. of unsalted Butter

Preparation Instructions:

Preparing the Crust:

1. With parchment paper, cover a 9-inch baking pan.
2. Process the sliced almonds and coconut in a food processor until they appear like grains of oatmeal. Set aside.
3. Add the vanilla extract, yacón syrup, sweetener, and butter over medium heat in a medium saucepan and thoroughly whisk to mix well. Remove from heat.
4. Add the almonds, salt, almond flour and coconut. Stir well. Place about two-thirds of the mixture in the baking pan.

To Make the Filling and Assemble:

1. Allow the cream to simmer over medium heat. Remove from heat and add the butter and chopped chocolate. Allow to melt for four minutes.
2. Add the vanilla extract and sweetener. Whisk the mixture until smooth.
3. Pour the filling on top of the crust. Sprinkle the rest of the crust mixture on top and refrigerate for 1 hour to firm up.
4. Remove the parchment paper and slice into 16 bars.

Macros: Fat: 25.5g | Carbs: 6.5g | Protein: 4.4g | Erythritol: 15g | Fiber: 3.2g | Calories: 275

02. No-Bake Peanut Butter Caramel Cookies

Preparation time: 5 minutes
Cook time: 10 minutes
Servings: 16
Ingredients:
- ¾ cup of creamy, salted Peanut Butter
- 1 cup Caramel Sauce
- ½ Vanilla extract or tsp Caramel
- ¾ cup of sliced Almonds
- ¾ cup unsweetened Flaked Coconut
- ¼ cup powdered Erythritol-based Sweetener
- 3 oz. of finely crushed Pork Rinds

Preparation Instructions:
01. Line the baking sheet using parchment or wax paper.
02. Stir the peanut butter and the caramel over low heat in a saucepan until smooth and melted. Stir the extract and remove from heat after stirring.
03. Pulse the sliced almonds and flaked coconut together in a food processor until the mixture appears like an oatmeal.
04. Add the almond mixture and coconut plus the sweetener, and crushed pork rinds. Stir to incorporate.
05. Using rounded tbsp., drop the mixture on the top of a coated baking sheet. Leave 2 inches in between them. Use palm to flatten the cookies.
06. Place in the refrigerator for an hour to firm.

Macros: Fat: 16.6g | Carbs: 5.1g | Protein: 7.3g | Erythritol: 9.4g | Fiber: 1.7g | Calories: 200

03. Sugar Cookie Bars

Preparation time: 15 minutes
Cook time: 18 minutes
Servings: 16
Ingredients:
Bar Ingredients:
- 2 tbsp. of Coconut flour
- 200g (2 cups) blanched Almond flour
- ½ cup of granulated Erythritol-based Sweetener
- ½ tsp. of baking powder
- ½ tsp. of Vanilla extract
- 1 large egg
- ¼ tsp. of salt
- 1 stick (½ cup) unsalted Butter, melted

Vanilla Frosting:
- ¼ cup (2 oz.) of softened Cream Cheese
- ½ cup (1 stick) of unsalted Butter
- ½ cup powdered Erythritol-based Sweetener
- 2-4 tbsp. of heavy Whipping Cream kept at room temp
- ½ tsp. of Vanilla extract
- 1 tbsp. of Coconut Sprinkles

Preparation Instructions:
Preparing the Bars:
1. Heat the oven to 325°F and grease a nine-inch baking pan.
2. Whisk the baking powder, salt, sweetener, vanilla extract egg, and butter in a large bowl until it is well mixed.
3. Evenly spread the dough in greased baking pan and Bake for 18 minutes until the sides appear golden brown. At this point the middle will remain soft. Take out of the oven and allow to completely cool in the pan.

Preparing the Assemble and Frosting:
4. Beat in cream cheese and butter using an electric mixer in a medium bowl until smooth. Add the powdered sweetener and beat.
5. Add 1 tbsp. of the heavy cream until frosting becomes spreadable. Beat in the vanilla extract until well incorporated.
6. Evenly spread frosting on the top of the cookie and make sure to garnish with coconut sprinkles. Slice into 16 bars.

Macros: Fat: 20.5g | Carbs: 3.9g | Protein: 3.9g | Erythritol: 15g | Fiber: 1.8g |Calories: 218

04. Dairy-Free Peanut Butter Bars

Preparation time: 15 minutes
Cook time: 5 minutes
Servings: 16

Ingredients:

Bar Ingredients:

- 2 tbsp. plus ½ cup of coconut oil
- ¾ cup of salted Creamy Peanut Butter
- ⅔ cup of powdered Erythritol-based Sweetener
- 1 tsp Vanilla extract
- 200g (2 cups) of defatted Peanut flour

Chocolate Glaze Ingredients:

- 3 oz. of sugarless dark chopped Chocolate
- 1 tbsp. of Coconut oil

Preparation Instructions:

Preparing the Bars:

1. Line a 9-inch baking pan using parchment paper.
2. Mix the coconut oil and peanut butter in a large bowl. Thoroughly whisk the mixture until smooth. Stir in vanilla extract and sweetener until it becomes thoroughly mixed.
3. Add the peanut flour and stir so that the dough sticks close. Firmly press the dough and evenly flatten it on a coated baking pan. Cover with parchment or wax paper.

Preparing the Assemble and Glaze:

1. Place the coconut oil and the chocolate in a microwaveable bowl. In 30-second increments, microwave on high power until smooth and melted.
2. Pour the glaze on the top of the bars and with a knife, spread it to the sides. Refrigerate for about an hour so that the chocolate becomes set.
3. Cut into sixteen bars.

Macros: Fat: 19g | Carbs: 7.2g | Protein: 5.5g | Erythritol: 11g | Fiber: 2.9g | Calories: 211

FROZEN DESSERTS

05. Vanilla Bean Semifreddo

Preparation time: 10 minutes
Cook time: 7 minutes
Servings: 3

Ingredients:
- 3 large egg yolks
- 2 large eggs
- 1 tbsp Vodka, divided (optional)
- ⅔ cup powdered Erythritol-based Sweetener
- ½ cup of Vanilla Beans
- ½ tsp Vanilla extract
- 1⅓ cups heavy Whipping Cream

Preparation Instructions:
1. Set a pan over a heatproof bowl and place the 2 large eggs, 3 egg yolks and ⅓ cup of the sweetener in water that is barely simmering. For 5-7 minutes, whisk the mixture of the egg yolk and the egg until it becomes thick. Take the bowl out of the pan and allow to cool while continuing to whisk it.
2. If you are using vodka, whisk it in. Cut open the vanilla bean and remove its seed with a sharp knife. Stir in the vanilla seeds.
3. Whip the cream plus the vanilla extract and the rest of the sweetener using an electric beater until mixture holds stiff peaks. Add the egg mixture and fold it gently until no streaks remain.
4. Transfer the mixture to an airtight container and freeze until firm, 6 to 8 hours.

06. Salted Caramel Affogato

Preparation time: 5 minutes
Cook time: 0 minutes
Servings: 1

Ingredients:
- ½ cup of Vanilla Beans
- ¼ cup of strong brewed coffee or 1 shot of freshly prepared espresso
- 2 tbsp. of salted Caramel Sauce

Preparation Instructions:
Inside a mug or a small bowl, place the semifreddo plus the caramel sauce. Make sure to heat the coffee prior and pour it over the top. Serve and enjoy!

07. Chocolate Fat Bomb Ice cream

Preparation time: 30 minutes
Cook time: 5 minutes
Servings: 2

Ingredients:
- 2½ cups of divided heavy Whipping Cream
- ½ stick (¼ cup) of Butter that is unsalted
- ⅔ cup of powdered Erythritol-based Sweetener
- 3 oz. of unsweetened chopped chocolate
- 1 tsp. of Vanilla extract
- A pinch of salt
- 2 tbsp. of vodka (optional)

Preparation Instructions:
1. Measure out 1½ cup of the Whipping cream into a large saucepan over medium heat. Add the butter just before it begins simmering and stir until the butter melts.
2. Remove from heat and include salt, vanilla extract, chocolate and the sweetener. Allow it to remain for about 5 minutes so that all the chocolate melts. Whisk until smooth and room temperature.
3. If you are using vodka, whisk it in and the rest of the 1 cup of cream. Refrigerate for 1-2 hours until it becomes cool to touch.
4. Transfer into an ice maker and churn using the manufacturer's instructions. Place in an airtight container and refrigerate until it becomes firm.

08. Frozen Key Lime Mini Pies

Preparation time: 20 minutes
Cook time: 7 minutes.
Servings: 6

Ingredients:

- ¼ cup plus 2 tbsp. of ground Erythritol-based Sweetener
- ½ cup (4 oz.) of softened Cream Cheese
- ½ cup of heavy Whipping Cream
- ⅓ cup of divided Key Lime juice
- ½ cup of finely sliced raw Pecans
- 1 tbsp. of butter (unsalted or salted)
- 1 tbsp. of granulated Erythritol-based Sweetener
- ¼ tsp. of salt

Preparation Instructions:

1. Coat six muffin cups using silicone liners or parchment paper.
2. Beat the lime juice, ¼ cup of ground sweetener and cream cheese using an electric mixer until smooth.
3. In a separate bowl, beat the cream with the rest of the ground sweetener until the mixture starts to hold stiff peaks. Fold the whipped cream into the cream cheese mixture. Pour mixture into the coated muffin cups.
4. In a small skillet, melt the butter over medium heat. Add the granulated sweetener and pecans and heat for 5-7 minutes until the pecans are fragrant and toasted. Remove from heat and sprinkle with salt and allow to cool for 5 minutes.
5. Sprinkle pecans on top.
6. Refrigerate for 3-4 hours to freeze.

09. Easy Root Beer Floats

Preparation time: 1-2 Hours
Cook time: 0 minutes
Servings: 2

Ingredients:

- 1 (12 oz.) bottle or can of chilled sugar-free root beer
- ½ cup of Whipped Cream

Preparation Instructions:

1. Line a baking sheet with parchment paper or wax paper. Place the whipped cream by heaping spoonful of the cream on the top of the paper and Refrigerate for 1-2 hours until it becomes firm.
2. With great care, peel the paper off the frozen whipped cream and divide between 2 ten-oz. glasses. Pour root beer into the glasses.

BROWNIES AND BOMBS

10. Healthy 1-Minute Low-carb Brownie

Preparation time: 2 minutes
Cook time: 1 Minute
Servings: 1

Ingredients:

- 1 scoop (32-34 grams) of chocolate protein powder, or 1 tbsp of coconut flour
- 1 tbsp granulated sweetener
- ½ tsp of baking powder
- 1 tbsp cocoa powder
- 1 whole egg or egg white
- ¼ cup milk of choice
- 1 tbsp of chocolate chunks

Preparation Instructions:

1. Grease an oven safe ramekin or small microwave-safe bowl using cooking spray and set aside.
2. Combine all dry ingredients in a medium bowl and mix very well. Add milk, chocolate chunks and egg white and thoroughly mix. Continue to add milk when you think the mixture is too thick; add the milk one spoon at a time until desired batter thickness is achieved.
3. Microwave in 30-second intervals or bake at 350 F for 12-15 minutes.

11. Chocolate Hazelnut Brownie Pie

Preparation time: 10 minutes
Cook time: 30 minutes
Servings: 8

Ingredients:

- ¾ cup of granulated Erythritol-based Sweetener
- 4 oz. of coarsely chopped unsweetened Chocolate
- 4 large eggs
- ½ cup of boiling Water
- 1 tsp Vanilla extract
- 100g (1 cup) Hazelnut meal
- 1 stick (½ cup) unsalted Butter

Preparation Instructions:

1. Heat the oven to 350° F. Grease a 9-inch ceramic pie pan or glass.
2. Pulse the sweetener and the chopped chocolate in a food processor. Carefully pour in boiling water while the food processor is running on high until the chocolate becomes smooth and melted.
3. Add the vanilla extract, butter, and eggs and process until it is well mixed. Fold in the hazelnut and process to make sure it well combined.
4. Pour batter into greased pan and bake for 25-30 minutes so that the middle becomes somewhat wet but the sides becomes finely set. Take it out of the oven and cool. Refrigerate for 2 hours.
5. Garnish with toasted hazelnuts and whipped cream.

Macros: Fat: 28.4g | Carbs: 6.8g |Protein: 7.3g | Erythritol: 22.5g | Fiber: 3.9g | Calories: 324

12. Coconut Milk Fudge Pops

Preparation time: 10 minutes
Cook time: 5 minutes
Servings: 6

Ingredients:

- ⅓ cup of Cocoa powder
- A pinch of salt
- 1½ tsp. of Vanilla extract
- 1 (13.5 oz.) can Full-Fat Coconut
- ⅓ cup of powdered Erythritol-based Sweetener

Preparation Instructions:

1. Place a semi-large saucepan over medium heat and whisk the salt, sweetener, cocoa powder, and coconut milk together. Allow it to simmer and continue whisking the mixture until it is even.
2. Let it simmer for 4-5 minutes, and keep whisking until the mixture becomes thick. Add the vanilla extract and whisk. Allow it to cool for ten minutes. After that, pour into the ice pop molds.
3. Refrigerate for one hour. Insert a stick into each mold at about two-thirds of the length of each mold.
4. For no fewer than 5 hours, freeze until it becomes solid. Run under hot water for 20-30 seconds to unmold. Gently twist the stick to release.

COOKIES

13. Slice-and-Bake Vanilla Wafers

Preparation time: 10 minutes
Cook time: 15 minutes
Servings: 2

Ingredients:

* 175g (1¾ cups) blanched Almond flour
* ½ cup granulated Erythritol-based Sweetener
* 1 stick (½ cup) unsalted softened Butter
* 2 tbsp. of Coconut flour
* ¼ tsp. of salt
* ½ tsp. of Vanilla extract

Preparation Instructions:

1.   Beat the sweetener and butter using an electric mixer in a large bowl for 2 minutes until it becomes fluffy and light. Then beat in the salt, vanilla extract, coconut flour, and almond until thoroughly mixed.
2.   Evenly spread the dough between two sheets of parchment or wax paper and wrap each portion into a size with a diameter of about 1½ inches. Then wrap in paper and refrigerate for 1-2 hours.
3.   Heat the oven to 325° F and line a baking sheet using silicone baking mats or parchment paper. Slice the dough into ¼- inch slices using a sharp knife. Put the sliced dough on the baking sheets and make sure to leave a 1-inch space between wafers.
4.   Place in the oven for about 5 minutes. Slightly flatten the cookies using a flat-bottomed glass. Bake for another 8-10 minutes.

Macros: Protein: 2.2g | Fat: 9.3g | Carbs: 2.5g | Erythritol: 6g | Fiber: 1.3g | Calories: 101

14. Amaretti

Preparation time: 15 minutes
Cook time: 22 minutes
Servings: 2

Ingredients:

* ½ cup of granulated Erythritol-based Sweetener
* 165g (2 cups) sliced Almonds
* ¼ cup of powdered of Erythritol-based sweetener
* 4 large egg whites
* Pinch of salt
* ½ tsp almond extract

Preparation Instructions:

1.   Heat the oven to 300° F and use parchment paper to line 2 baking sheets. Grease the parchment slightly.
2.   Process the powdered sweetener, granulated sweetener, and sliced almonds in a food processor until it appears like coarse crumbs.
3.   Beat the egg whites plus the salt and almond extracts using an electric mixer in a large bowl until they hold soft peaks. Fold in the almond mixture so that it becomes well combined.
4.   Drop spoonfuls of the dough onto the prepared baking sheet and allow for a space of 1 inch between them. Press a sliced almond into the top of each cookie.
5.   Bake in the oven for 22 minutes until the sides becomes brown. They will appear jellylike when they are taken out from the oven but will begin to be firms as it cools down.

Macros: Fat: 8.8g | Carbs: 4.1g | Protein: 5.3g | Fiber: 2.3g | Erythritol: 18g| Calories: 117

15. Peanut Butter Cookies for Two

Preparation time: 5 minutes
Cook time: 12 minutes
Servings: 1

Ingredients:

- 1½ tbsp. of creamy salted Peanut Butter
- 1 tbsp. of unsalted softened Butter
- 2 tsp. of lightly beaten egg
- 2 tbsp. of granulated Erythritol-based Sweetener
- ¼ tsp. of Vanilla extract
- 2 tbsp. of defatted Peanut flour
- Pinch of salt
- 2 tsp. of sugarless Chocolate Chips
- ⅛ tsp. of baking powder

Preparation Instructions:

1. Heat the oven to 325° F and line a baking sheet with a silicone baking mat or parchment paper.
2. Beat in the sweetener, butter, and peanut butter using an electric mixer in a small bowl until it is thoroughly mixed. Then beat in the vanilla extract and the egg.
3. Add the salt, baking powder, and peanut flour and mix until the dough clumps together. Cut the dough into two and shape each of them into a ball.
4. Position the dough ball into the coated baking sheets and flatten into a circular shape about ½ inch thick. Garnish the dough tops with a tsp. of chocolate chips. Gently press them into the dough to stick.
5. Bake for 10-12 minutes until golden brown.

Macros: Fat: 13.2g | Carbs: 5.7g | Protein: 4.9g | Erythritol: 16g |Fiber: 1.9g | Calories: 163

16. Cream Cheese Cookies

Preparation time: 15 minutes
Cook time: 12 minutes
Servings: 6

Ingredients:

- ¼ cup (½ stick) unsalted softened Butter
- ½ cup (4 oz.) of softened Cream Cheese
- 1 large egg at room temp
- ½ of cup granulated Erythritol-based Sweetener
- 150g (1½ cups) of blanched Almond flour
- 1 tsp. of baking Powder
- ½ tsp. of Vanilla extract
- Powdered Erythritol-based sweetener (for dusting)
- ¼ tsp. of salt

Preparation Instructions:

1. Heat the oven to 350°F and line with a silicone baking mat or parchment paper.
2. Beat the butter and cream cheese using an electric mixer in a large bowl until it appears smooth. Add the sweetener and keep beating. Beat in the vanilla extract and the egg.
3. Whisk in the salt, baking powder, and almond flour in a medium bowl. Add the flour mixture into the cream cheese and until well incorporated.
4. Drop the dough in spoonfuls onto the coated baking sheet. Flatten the cookies.
5. Bake for 10-12 minutes. Dust with powdered sweetener when cool.

Macros: Fat: 13.7g | Carbs: 3.4g | Protein: 4.1g | Erythritol: 10g | Fiber: 1.5g | Calories: 154

17. Chewy Double Chocolate Cookies

Preparation time: 15 minutes
Cook time: 12 minutes
Servings: 10

Ingredients:

- 3 tbsp. of Cocoa powder
- 2 tbsp. of (88g) plus ¾ cup blanched Almond flour
- ½ tsp. of baking soda
- 1 tbsp. of grass-fed Gelatin
- ½ tsp. of salt
- ½ stick (¼ cup) unsalted softened Butter
- ½ cup of granulated Erythritol-based sweetener
- 1 large egg at room temp
- ¼ cup of unsalted Creamy Almond Butter
- ½ tsp. of Vanilla extract
- ⅓ cup sugarless Chocolate Chips

Preparation Instructions:

1. Heat the oven to 350° F and line 2 baking sheets with silicone baking mats or parchment paper.
2. Whisk the gelatin, salt, baking soda, cocoa powder, and almond flour together in a medium bowl.
3. Beat the sweetener, almond butter, and butter with an electric mixer in a large bowl until it is thoroughly mixed. Beat the vanilla extract and the egg. The beat in the almond mixture so that the dough sticks together. Add the chocolate chips and stir.
4. Roll the dough into medium-sized cookies and space them an inch apart. Flatten to about ½ inch thick
5. Bake for about 12 minutes.

Macros: Fat: 15.1g | Carbs: 6.9g |Protein: 5.5g | Erythritol: 12g | Fiber: 3.4g | Calories: 180

PIES AND TARTS

18. Mocha Cream Pie

Preparation time: 15 minutes
Cook time: 5 minutes
Servings: 10

Ingredients:

- 1 cup strongly brewed Coffee at room temp
- 1 Easy Chocolate Pie Crust
- 1 cup heavy Whipping Cream
- 1½ tsp. of grass-fed Gelatin
- 1 tsp. of Vanilla extract
- ¼ cup Cocoa powder
- ½ cup powdered Erythritol-based Sweetener

Preparation Instructions:

1. Grease a 9-inch glass pie pan or ceramic. Press the crust mixture evenly and firmly to the sides of the greased pan or its bottom. Refrigerate until the filling is prepared.
2. Pour the coffee in a small saucepan and add gelatin. Whisk thoroughly and then place over medium heat. Allow to simmer, whisking from time to time to make sure the gelatin dissolves. Allow to cool for 20 minutes.
3. Add the vanilla extract, cocoa powder, sweetener, and the cream into a large bowl. Use an electric mixer to beat to that it holds stiff peaks.
4. Add gelatin mixture that has been cooled and then beat until it is well incorporated. Pour over the cooled crust and place in the refrigerator for 3 hours until it becomes firm.

Macros: Fat: 20.2g | Carbs: 6.2g | Protein: 4.7g | Erythritol: 18g |Fiber: 3.1g | Calories: 218

19. Coconut Custard Pie

Preparation time: 10 minutes
Cook time: 50 minutes
Servings: 8

Ingredients:

- 1 cup of heavy Whipping Cream
- ¾ cup of powdered Erythritol-based Sweetener
- ½ cup of full-fat Coconut Milk
- 4 large eggs
- ½ stick (¼ cup) of cooled, unsalted, melted butter
- 1¼ cups of unsweetened shredded coconut
- 3 tbsp. of Coconut flour
- ½ tsp. of baking powder
- ½ tsp. of Vanilla extract
- ¼ tsp. of salt

Preparation Instructions:

1. Heat the oven to 350° F and grease a 9-inch ceramic pie pan or glass.
2. Place the melted butter, eggs, coconut milk, sweetener, and cream in a blender. Blend well.
3. Add the vanilla extract, baking powder, salt, coconut flour, and a cup of shredded coconut. Continue blending.
4. Empty the mixture into the pie pan and sprinkle with the rest of the shredded coconut. Bake for 40-50 minutes and stop when the center is until jiggly but the sides are set.
5. Take out of the oven and allow it to cool for 30 minutes. Place in the refrigerator and allow to stay for 2 hours before cutting it.

Macros: Fat: 29.5g | Carbs: 6.7g | Protein: 5.3g | Erythritol: 22.5g |Fiber: 2.6g | Calories: 317

20. Dairy-Free Fruit Tarts

Preparation time: 15 minutes
Cook time: 15 mins
Servings: 2

Ingredients:

- 1 cup Coconut Whipped Cream
- ½ Easy Shortbread Crust (dairy-free option)
- Fresh mint Sprigs
- ½ cup mixed fresh Berries

Preparation Instructions:

1. Grease two 4" pans with detachable bottoms. Pour the shortbread mixture into pans and firmly press into the edges and bottom of each pan. Refrigerate for 15 minutes.
2. Loosen the crust carefully to remove from the pan.
3. Distribute the whipped cream between the tarts and evenly spread to the sides. Refrigerate for 1-2 hours to make it firm.
4. Use the berries and sprig of mint to garnish each of the tarts

Macros: Fat: 28.9g | Carbs: 8.3g | Protein: 5.8g | Erythritol: 22.5g | Fiber: 3g | Calories: 306

21. Strawberry Rhubarb Crisp for Two

Preparation time: 10 minutes
Cook time: 30 minutes
Servings: 2

Ingredients:

Topping Ingredients:

- 1 tbsp. of unsweetened shredded Coconut
- 2½ tbsp. of blanched Almond flour
- 1½ tsp. of finely chopped Pecans
- 1 tbsp. of granulated Erythritol-based Sweetener

Pinch of salt

- 2 tsp. melted unsalted Butter
- ¼ tsp. of ground Cinnamon

Filling Ingredients:

- ⅓ cup of sliced fresh Strawberries
- ½ cup of chopped fresh Rhubarb
- 1/16 tsp. of Xanthan Gum
- 1 tbsp. of granulated Erythritol-based Sweetener

Preparation Instructions:

1. Preparing the Topping Ingredients:
2. Heat the oven to 300° F and line a baking sheet with parchment paper.
3. Whisk the cinnamon, pecans, salt, sweetener, coconut, and almond flour in a medium bowl. Add the melted butter into the mixture and stir until the resulting mixture appears like coarse crumbs.
4. Place on the coated baking sheet and firmly press down to make it flat. Bake for 15 minutes then allow it to cool.
5. Preparing the Filling and Assembling Ingredients:
6. Heat the oven to 400° F
7. Add all the filling ingredients in a medium bowl and make sure that you thoroughly mix them. Place into an 8-oz ramekin and cover with foil. Place in the oven to bake for 10-15 minutes.

Macros: Calories: 135 | Fat: 11.5g | Protein: 2.6g | Carbs: 6.3g | Fiber: 2.6g | Erythritol: 15g

OTHER DELICIOUS DESSERTS

22. Raspberry Fool

Preparation time: 15 minutes
Cook time: 0 minutes
Servings: 4

Ingredients:

- 2-4 tbsp. of powdered and divided Erythritol-based Sweetener
- 1 cup of thawed frozen Raspberries
- Fresh berries, for garnish
- 1 cup of Whipped Cream

Preparation Instructions:

1. Process 2 tbsp. of sweetener and berries in a food processor or blender until smooth.
2. Fold in the raspberry puree, leaving some streaks.
3. Pour mixture into four dessert cups.
4. Garnish with the berries.

Macros: Fat: 20.1g | Carbs: 5.2g |Protein: 1.7g | Erythritol: 15g |Fiber: 1g | Calories: 226

23. Cannoli Dessert Dip

Preparation time: 10 minutes
Cook time: —
Servings: 8

Ingredients:

- ¾ cup (6 oz.) of softened Cream Cheese
- 1 cup of whole-milk Ricotta Cheese at room temp
- ½ tsp. of Vanilla extract
- ¾ cup of powdered Erythritol-based Sweetener, plus an additional amount for sprinkling
- ⅓ cup Sugarless Chocolate Chips
- ½ cup of heavy Whipping Cream

Preparation Instructions:

1. Blend the vanilla extract, sweetener, cream cheese, and ricotta in a food processor or blender until smooth.
2. Whisk in the cream using an electric mixer in a medium bowl until it holds solid peaks. Carefully fold in the chocolate chips and the ricotta mixture and save some for later to sprinkle on top.

Macros: Fat: 17.9g | Carbs: 5.6g | Protein: 5.7g | Erythritol: 22.5g | Fiber: 1.3g | Calories: 219

24. Slow Cooker Coffee Coconut Custard

Preparation time: 5 minutes
Cook time: 2 hours
Servings: 4

Ingredients:
- 1 large egg
- 2 tbsp. of plus 1 cup of Full-Fat Coconut Milk
- ½ tsp. of Vanilla extract
- 2 large egg yolks
- 1 tsp. of Espresso powder
- ½ cup of powdered Erythritol-based Sweetener

Preparation Instructions:
1. Whisk all the ingredients in a medium bowl until the espresso powder dissolves.
2. Pour into 4-oz. coffee cups or ramekins and place in a slow cooker.
3. Fill up the slow cooker with water so that it goes halfway up the edges of the ramekins. Do not allow water to get into the custard.
4. Place over high heat for 1½-2 hours and stop when the middle is lightly jiggly but the custard is set.
5. Remove from the heat and allow to cool to room temp. Afterwards, refrigerate for 2 hours. Remove and serve.

Macros: Fat: 16.8g | Carbs: 2.6g | Protein: 4.3g | Erythritol: 30g |Fiber: 0g | Calories: 186

25. Coconut Lime Panna Cotta

Preparation time: 10 minutes
Cook time: 5 minutes
Servings: 4

Ingredients:
- 1½ tsp. of grass-fed Gelatin
- 13.5-oz. (or 1) of can Full-Fat Coconut Milk
- 1 tsp. of grated Lime Zest
- ⅓ cup of powdered Erythritol-based Sweetener
- ¼ tsp. of Coconut extract
- 2 tbsp. of fresh Lime Juice

Preparation Instructions:
1. Grease four 4-oz. ramekins.
2. Whisk in the gelatin plus half of the coconut milk in a saucepan and place over medium heat. Allow to simmer and keep whisking until the gelatin dissolves.
3. Remove from heat and add the coconut extract, lime juice, lime zest, sweetener, and the rest of the coconut milk. Whisk to mix thoroughly and dissolve the sweetener.
4. Divide the mixture between the greased ramekins to refrigerate for 3 hours until it sets.
5. Place the ramekins in a dish of hot water for 20-30 seconds to unmold. Position the plate upside down on the top of the ramekins and turn everything over. Shake it thoroughly to free it

Macros: Fat: 18.5g | Carbs: 3.2g | Protein: 2.6g | Erythritol: 19.9g | Fiber: 0g | Calories: 190

26. Chocolate Cobbler

Preparation time: 10 minutes
Cook time: 40 minutes
Servings: 8
Ingredients:
Chocolate Layer Ingredients:
- ⅓ cup granulated Erythritol-based Sweetener
- 1¼ cups blanched Almond flour
- ¼ cup Cocoa powder
- 3 tbsp. of unflavored Whey Protein powder
- 2 tsp. of baking powder
- ½ tsp. of Espresso powder
- ¼ tsp. of salt
- ½ stick (¼ cup) of unsalted melted Butter
- ½ cup of heavy Whipping Cream

Topping Ingredients:
- 1 tbsp. of Cocoa powder
- ¾ cup of hot Water
- 2 tbsp. of granulated Erythritol-based Sweetener

Preparation Instructions:
1. Heat the oven to 325° F.
2. Preparing the chocolate layer: Whisk the baking powder, salt, espresso powder, protein powder, cocoa powder, sweetener, and almond flour in a large bowl until it is well mixed. In an 8-inch baking dish, evenly spread the mixture.
3. Preparing the topping: Whisk the cocoa powder and the sweetener together in a small bowl. Evenly sprinkle on the top of the cobbler. Empty the hot water over the cobbler and make sure not to stir.
4. Place in an oven and bake for 35-40 minutes until the center is set.
5. Take out of the oven and allow to cool for 10-15 minutes. Serve warm.

Macros: Fat: 20g | Carbs: 7.1g | Protein: 6.5g | Erythritol: 13.7g | Fiber: 3.4g | Calories: 223

27. Easy Shortbread Crust

Preparation time: 5 minutes
Cook time: 0 minutes
Servings: 10
Ingredients:
- ¼ cup of powdered Erythritol-based Sweetener
- 150g (1½ cups) of blanched Almond flour
- ¼ cup (½ stick) of unsalted melted Butter
- ½ tsp. of salt

Preparation Instructions:
1. Whisk together the salt, sweetener, and almond flour in a medium dish.
2. Add the melted butter and stir until mixture starts to clump together.

Macros: Fat: 12.7g | Carbs: 3.6g | Protein: 3.7g | Erythritol: 6g | Fiber: 1.8g | Calories: 137

28. Easy Chocolate Pie Crust

Preparation time: 5 minutes
Cook time: 0 minutes
Servings: 10

Ingredients:
- ¼ cup Cocoa powder
- 125g (1¼ cups) of blanched Almond flour
- ¼ cup powdered Erythritol-based Sweetener
- ¼ tsp. of salt
- 1 tbsp. Water
- ¼ cup (½ stick) unsalted melted Butter

Preparation Instructions:
1. Whisk together the sweetener, salt, cocoa powder, and almond flour.
2. Add the water and melted butter and ensure to stir until mixture starts to clump together.

Macros: Fat: 11.6g | Carbs: 4.3g | Protein: 3.5g | Erythritol: 6g | Fiber: 2.3g | Calories: 126

29. Whipped Cream

Preparation time: 5 minutes
Cook time: 0 minutes
Servings: 2

Ingredients:
- 2 tbsp. of powdered Erythritol-based Sweetener
- ½ tsp. of Vanilla extract
- 1 cup of heavy Whipping Cream

Preparation Instructions:
Beat ingredients using an electric mixer in a larger bowl until it holds solid peaks.

Macros: Fat: 10.4g | Carbs: 0.9g | Protein: 0.6g | Erythritol: 3.8g |Fiber: 0g | Calories: 104

30. Coconut Whipped Cream

Preparation time: 8 minutes
Cook time: 0 minutes
Servings: 1

Ingredients:
- ½ tsp. of Vanilla or coconut extract
- 2 tbsp. of powdered Erythritol-based Sweetener
- 13.5 oz. (1 can) of Full-fat Coconut Milk, placed in a refrigerator overnight

Preparation Instructions:
1. Place the beaters and a mixing bowl in a fridge to chill for at least 10-15 minutes.
2. Skim the solid part of the coconut milk starting from the top of the can into the already chilled bowl. With an electric mixer, beat the coconut cream until it becomes light and smooth and have the ability to hold soft peaks.
3. Add the coconut extract and the sweetener and continue beating to thoroughly mix. The whipping cream will typically become firmer once placed in the refrigerator.

Macros: Fat: 18.5g | Carbs: 2.7g | Protein: 1.9g | Erythritol: 7.5g | Fiber: 0g | Calories: 184

31. Chocolate Buttercream Frosting

Preparation time: 10 minutes
Cook time: 0 minutes
Servings: 3

Ingredients:

- 1 tbsp. of Coconut oil
- 2 oz. of chopped unsweetened Chocolate
- 3 oz. of Cream cheese
- 1 stick (½ cup) unsalted softened Butter
- 2 tbsp. of Cocoa powder
- ⅔ cup of powdered Erythritol-based Sweetener
- ½ tsp Vanilla extract
- ¼-½ cup of heavy Whipping Cream at room temp

Preparation Instructions:

1. Combine the chocolate and coconut oil in a medium bowl. Microwave in 30-second increments, stirring each time until the mixture is smooth and melted. Set aside to allow it to cool.
2. Beat the cream cheese and butter in a large bowl until smooth. Beat in the cocoa powder and the sweetener until it is thoroughly mixed.
3. Add the vanilla extract and the melted chocolate and keep beating until smooth. At this point, the mixture will get thick.
4. Add two tbsp. of the cream, one at a time.

Macros: Fat: 15.2g | Carbs: 2.5g | Protein: 1.6g | Erythritol: 13.7g | Fiber: 1.1g | Calories: 161

32. Caramel

Preparation time: 5 minutes
Cook time: 10 minutes
Servings: 1

Ingredients:

- 2 tbsp. of plus ¼ cup of granulated Erythritol-based Sweetener
- ½ stick (¼ cup) of unsalted Butter
- ½ cup heavy Whipping Cream
- 2 tsp. of Yacón Syrup (optional though)
- ¼ tsp. of medium-grind Sea salt or Kosher
- 2 tbsp. of Water
- ¼ tsp. of Xanthan Gum

Preparation Instructions:

1. Melt the sweetener, yacón syrup and butter over medium heat in a medium saucepan until the sweetener becomes dissolved. Boil for 3-5 minutes until the color becomes deeper.
2. Remove from heat and add the cream. Sprinkle the mixture with xanthan gum and thoroughly mix. Add the salt at this time.
3. Place the mixture back over medium heat and allow to boil for a minute.

Macros: Fat: 10.8g | Carbs: 3.4g | Protein: 0.4g | Erythritol: 11.3g | Fiber: 0g | Calories: 113

33. Chocolate Peanut Butter Sauce for Two

Preparation time: 1 Minute
Cook time: 1 Minute
Servings: 1

Ingredients:
- 2 tbsp. of Creamy salted Peanut Butter
- 1½ tbsp. of unsalted Butter
- 1 tbsp. of powdered Erythritol-based Sweetener
- 2 tsp. of Cocoa powder
- ⅛ tsp. of Vanilla extract

Preparation Instructions:
1.   Place the butter and peanut butter in a medium sized bowl and melt in a high-powered microwave. Stir until smooth.
2.   Whisk in the vanilla extract, cocoa powder, and sweetener.

Macros: Fat: 15.9g | Carbs: 4.6g | Protein: 4g | Erythritol: 7.5g |Fiber: 1.5g | Calories: 177

34. Coconut Sprinkles

Preparation time: 1 Minute
Cook time: —
Servings: 1

Ingredients:
- 1 tbsp. of unsweetened shredded Coconut
- Food coloring

Preparation Instructions:
1.   Mix the coconut plus one or two drops of food coloring in a medium bowl until it is thoroughly mixed.
2.   Allow it to dry until you are ready to use it. Repeat the process with the additional coconut for any color sprinkles you desire.

Macros: Fat: 1.1g | Carbs: 0.4g | Protein: 0.1g | Fiber: 0.2g | Calories: 11

35. Chocolate Dessert Cups

Preparation time: 15 minutes
Cook time: 2 minutes
Servings: 6

Ingredients:
- 1½ tsp. of Coconut oil, or ¼ oz. Cacao Butter
- 2 oz. of dark chopped sugarless Chocolate

Preparation Instructions:
1.   Place the parchment paper or 12 mini silicone liners in a medium sized muffin pan.
2.   Place the cacao butter and chocolate in a bowl. Place in a high-powered microwave in thirty second increments. Make sure to stir after each increment until smooth and melted.
3.   Spoon the chocolate into each of the mini muffin coated cups.
4.   Place in the refrigerator for 30 minutes so that it becomes completely set.

Macros: Fat: 4.7g | Carbs: 3.8g | Protein: 0.5g | Erythritol: 2g | Fiber: 1.9g | Calories: 48

CANDY AND CONFECTIONS

36. Peppermint Patties

Preparation time: 20 minutes
Cook time: 5 minutes
Servings: 12

Ingredients:
- ½ cup of slightly softened Coconut oil
- 2 tbsp. of Coconut cream
- ½ cup of powdered Erythritol-based Sweetener
- 1 tsp. of Peppermint extract
- 3 oz. of sugarless chopped dark Chocolate
- 1 tbsp. of Coconut Oil or ½ oz. of Cacao Butter

Preparation Instructions:
1. Beat the coconut cream and coconut oil using an electric bowl in a medium bowl until smooth.
2. Add the peppermint extract and sweetener and keep beating.
3. Line a baking sheet with parchment or wax paper. Drop a heaping spoonful of the mixture on the parchment or wax paper. Make a circular shape about 1½ inches in diameter.
4. Refrigerate for 2 hours until it becomes firm.
5. Melt the cacao butter and chocolate together and put inside a bowl and place over a pan containing water that just started simmering. Keep stirring the mixture to make sure it is well mixed. Remove from heat.
6. Position the patties on the baking sheet. Then allow it to set.

Macros: Fat: 13.6g | Carbs: 2.9g | Protein: 0.4g | Erythritol: 11.5g | Fiber: 1.4g | Calories: 126

37. Maple Walnut Fudge Cups

Preparation time: 5 minutes
Cook time: 5 minutes
Servings: 12

Ingredients:
- 1 stick (½ cup) salted Butter
- 4 oz. of Coconut Butter
- ¼ cup of powdered Erythritol-based Sweetener
- 1 tsp. of Yacón Syrup (optional, for flavor and color)
- 2½ tsp. of Maple extract
- ¼ cup of toasted chopped Walnuts

Preparation Instructions:
1. Line a mini muffin pan using parchment paper or a 12-inch silicone liner.
2. Melt the coconut butter and butter over low heat in a medium saucepan. Stir well until smooth.
3. Whisk in the maple extract, yacón syrup, and the sweetener. Add the toasted walnuts and stir.
4. Pour mixture into the coated mini muffin cups and place in the refrigerator to firm up for 1 hour.

Macros: Fat: 14.7g | Carbs: 3.2g | Protein: 1.4g | Erythritol: 5g | Fiber: 1.9g | Calories: 150

38. Toffee Almond Bark

Preparation time: 5 minutes
Cook time: 15 minutes
Servings: 12

Ingredients:

- 2 tbsp. of salted Butter
- 3 tbsp. of granulated Erythritol-based Sweetener
- ¼ tsp. of Vanilla extract
- 1 cup of raw Almonds
- 1 tbsp coconut oil, or ½ oz. cacao butter
- 6 oz. of sugarless chopped dark chocolate
- Pinch of salt

Preparation Instructions:

1. Line a baking sheet with parchment paper.
2. Mix the butter and sweetener over medium heat in a medium saucepan. Stir well until the sweetener dissolves. Add the almonds and allow to boil. Cook for 5-7 minutes.
3. Remove from heat and stir in the salt and vanilla. Arrange the almonds in a single layer on the baking sheet and allow to cool for 20 minutes.
4. Melt the cacao butter and butter together over a pan of water that just began simmering in a heatproof bowl until smooth. Add the almonds and toss well to coat. Spread the mixture on the baking sheet.
5. Refrigerate for 30 minutes so that it becomes set. With fingers, break into pieces.

Macros: Fat: 13.9g | Carbs: 8.3g | Protein: 3.3g | Erythritol: 6.8 | Fiber: 4.3g | Calories: 153

39. Macadamia Coconut Truffles

Preparation time: 20 minutes
Cook time: 0 minutes
Servings: 12

Ingredients:

- 3 tbsp. plus ⅔ cup of unsweetened shredded coconut, divided
- 2 cups of roasted unsalted Macadamia nuts
- ⅓ cup of powdered Erythritol-based Sweetener
- 2 tbsp. of grass-fed Collagen powder
- 1 tbsp. of melted Coconut oil
- ⅛ tsp. of salt
- 1 tsp. of Vanilla extract

Preparation Instructions:

1. Place the ⅔ cup of shredded coconut and macadamia nuts in a food processor. Process the mixture on high until it starts to clump into a ball.
2. In a large bowl, add the vanilla extract, melted coconut oil, salt, collagen, and sweetener and thoroughly mix.
3. On a shallow plate, spread the rest of the 3 tbsp. of shredded coconut. Line a baking sheet with parchment or wax paper.
4. Working with a tbsp. at a time, crush the truffle mixture to compress it. Roll it into a ball. Roll each ball in the shredded coconut and position on the coated baking sheet. Place in the refrigerator for about an hour to firm it up.

Macros: Fat: 20.3g | Carbs: 4.3g | Protein: 2.1g | Erythritol: 6.6g | Fiber: 2.5g | Calories: 202

40. Peanut Butter and Jelly Cups

Preparation time: 5 minutes
Cook time: 10 minutes
Servings: 12

Ingredients:

- ¼ cup of Water
- ¾ cup of fresh Raspberries
- 6- 8 tbsp. of powdered Erythritol-based Sweetener, divided
- 1 tsp. of grass-fed Gelatin
- ⅔ cup of Coconut oil
- ⅔ cup of salted creamy Peanut Butter

Preparation Instructions:

1. Line muffin pan with parchment paper or 12-inch silicone liners.
2. Boil the water and the raspberries over medium heat in a medium saucepan and allow to simmer for 5 minutes. Use a fork to mash the raspberries.
3. Add the powdered sweetener and stir until it is well incorporated. Whisk the gelatin in and allow to cool as you are preparing the peanut butter mixture.
4. Mix the coconut oil and peanut butter in a microwaveable bowl for 30-60 seconds until it melts. Whisk the powdered sweeter in.
5. Spoon about one tbsp. of peanut butter mixture in each cup and place in the freezer for about 5 minutes to firm up.
6. Divide the raspberry mixture between the cups and garnish with the rest of the peanut butter mixture.
7. Refrigerate for 30 minutes.

Macros: Fat: 19.4g | Carbs: 4.4g | Protein: 3.6g | Erythritol: 10g | Fiber: 1.4g | Calories: 200

41. Watermelon Lime Gummies

Preparation time: 5 minutes
Cook time: 5 minutes
Servings: 6

Ingredients:

- ⅓ cup of fresh Lime Juice
- 1¼ cups of sugarless Watermelon-flavored beverage
- 2 tbsp. of powdered Erythritol-based Sweetener
- 3 tbsp. of grass-fed Gelatin
- Gummy mold or a mini silicone muffin pan (this is optional)

Preparation Instructions:

1. Mix the lime juice and watermelon beverage in a medium saucepan. Whisk in the sweetener and the gelatin and let it simmer. Stir to make sure that the gelatin dissolves. Add more sweetener to taste.
2. Remove from heat. Pour into the silicone molds. Place in the refrigerator for 2 hours to make it firmer.
3. Remove the gummies from the molds. Also, remove the parchment paper from the baking pan.

Macros: Fat: 0g | Carbs: 1.1g | Protein: 3.1g | Erythritol: 6.3g | Fiber: 0.1g | Calories: 17

CAKES

42. No-Bake Blueberry Cheesecake Bars

Preparation time: 15 minutes (not including crust)
Cook time: 7 minutes
Servings: 16

Ingredients:

Bar Ingredients:
- 2 (8-oz.) softened packages of Cream Cheese
- 1 Easy Shortbread Crust
- ¼ cup heavy whipping cream kept at room temp
- ½ cup of powdered Erythritol-based Sweetener
- 1 tsp grated Lemon Zest

Topping Ingredients:
- ¼ cup of Water
- 1 cup of Blueberries
- 1 tbsp fresh Lemon juice
- ¼ cup of powdered Erythritol-based Sweetener
- ¼ tsp Xanthan gum for garnish (optional)

Preparation Instruction:

Preparing the Bars:

1. Firmly press the crust mixture of the shortbread into the bottom of a baking pan. Place the crust in the refrigerator.
2. Melt the chocolate in a bowl that you've set over a pan that is placed on a water that just began simmering. Take the bowl out of the pan and allow it to cool for about 10 minutes.
3. With an electric mixer, beat the sweetener and the butter for 2 minutes until it is well incorporated and fluffy. Carefully add the melted chocolate while the mixer is running and continue beating until smooth. Add the salt, espresso powder, and vanilla extract.
4. Add in the eggs one after the other and continue beating for 5 minutes. Carefully pour the filling ingredients on the top of the chilled crust and make sure to smoothen the top. Refrigerate for 2 hours.

Garnishing the Bars:

Carefully spread the whipped cream and chocolate on top.

Macros: Fat: 23.7g | Carbs: 4.6g | Protein: 4.6g | Erythritol: 15g | Fiber: 2.2g | Calories: 255

43. Strawberry Cheesecake Pops

Preparation time: 10 minutes
Cook time: 0 minutes
Servings: 6

Ingredients:
- ½ cup of heavy Whipping Cream
- ½ cup (4 oz.) of softened Cream Cheese
- 1 tsp. of grated Lemon Zest
- 2 tbsp. plus ¼ cup of powdered Erythritol-based Sweetener
- 1 cup of chopped strawberries, (divided)
- 2 tsp. of fresh Lemon Juice

Preparation Instructions:
1. Place the cream cheese inside a high-powered blender or a food processor and process until the cream becomes smooth.
2. Add the lemon juice, lemon zest, sweetener, and cream. Process until well mixed.
3. Add the strawberries (¾ cup) and process until becomes very smooth. Stir in the rest of the sliced strawberries.
4. Transfer the mixture the ice pop and insert a stick about two-thirds into each of the mold.
5. Refrigerate for 4 hours or more. Place for 20-30 seconds under hot water to unmold. Gently twist the stick to release.

44. Chocolate-Covered Cheesecake Bites

Preparation time: 20 minutes
Cook time: 5 minutes
Servings: 12

Ingredients:
- 1 (8 oz.) package of softened Cream Cheese
- ½ stick (¼ cup) unsalted softened Butter
- ½ cup of powdered Erythritol-based Sweetener
- ½ tsp. of vanilla extract
- 4 oz. of sugarless chopped dark Chocolate
- 1½ tbsp. of Coconut oil or ¾ oz. of Cacao Butter

Preparation Instructions:
1. Line a baking sheet with parchment or wax paper.
2. Beat the butter and cream cheese with an electric mixer in a large bowl until it is thoroughly mixed. Beat in the vanilla extract and sweetener until smooth.
3. Form the mixture into 1-inch balls and position on the coated baking sheet. Place them in the fridge for 3-4 hours until it becomes firm.
4. Melt the cacao butter and chocolate together over water that just began simmering over a heatproof bowl. Stir until mixture becomes smooth. Remove from heat.
5. Dunk each ball into melted chocolate. Coat well and remove using a fork. Firmly tap the fork on the sides of the bowl to eliminate extra chocolate.
6. Position the ball on the baking sheet and let it set. Do the same for the rest of the cheesecake balls.
7. Decoratively sprinkle the rest of the chocolate over the lined balls.

Macros: Fat: 13.5g | Carbs: 5.2g | Protein: 1.7g | Erythritol: 12g | Fiber: 2.2g | Calories: 148

45. Tiramisu Sheet Cake

Preparation time: 25 minutes
Cook time: 22 minutes
Servings: 20
Ingredients:
Cake Ingredients:
- ¾ cup granulated Erythritol-based Sweetener
- 200g (2 cups) of blanched Almond flour
- ⅓ cup of unflavored Whey Protein powder
- 37g (⅓ cup) of Coconut flour
- 1 tbsp. of baking Powder
- ½ tsp. of salt
- 1 stick (½ cup) of unsalted and melted Butter
- ¾ cup of unsweetened Almond Milk
- 1 tsp. of Vanilla extract
- 3 large eggs
- 1 tbs. of dark Rum (optional)
- ¼ cup of cooled strong brewed coffee or espresso

Mascarpone Frosting Ingredients:
- 4 oz. (½ cup) of softened Cream Cheese
- 8 oz. of softened Mascarpone Cheese
- 1 tsp. of Vanilla extract
- ½-⅔ cup of heavy Whipping cream kept at room temp
- ½ cup of powdered Erythritol-based Sweetener

Ingredients for Garnishing:
- 1-oz. of sugarless dark Chocolate
- 1 tbsp. of Cocoa powder

Preparation Instructions:
1. In a blender or food processor, grind the macadamia nuts to a fine texture.
2. Add all the cinnamon roll ingredients with the exception of for caramel sauce, and then put in the refrigerator to chill for an hour.
3. Heat the oven to 350° F. Line a baking tray with parchment paper.
4. Roll out the dough and make a large rectangle shape on a parchment-lined surface.
5. Spread Keto Caramel Sauce over the batter.
6. Carefully roll the dough into a log shape and seal the edge.
7. Place a sharp knife in a warm water and cut the log into about 10-12 rolls.
8. Position rolls on coated tray and place in the oven for 25 to 30 minutes, making sure that you check after 20 minutes to check if it is cooked through.
9. While the cinnamon rolls are baking in the oven, make the glaze. Combine all ingredients in a blender or mixing bowl.
10. Take keto cinnamon rolls out of the oven. Let it cool before you glaze. You can serve warm with glaze garnished on the top.

Macros: Calories: 477 | Fat: 45.6g | Carbs: 17.1g | Fiber: 7.1g | Protein: 5.6g

46. Cinnamon Crumb Cake Keto Donuts

Preparation time: 10 minutes
Cook time: 15 minutes
Servings: 1

Ingredients:

- ½ cup of Coconut flour
- ¼ cup of Almond flour
- 1 tbsp of Flaxseed meal
- 1 tsp of baking powder
- ¼ tsp salt
- 1 tsp of Cinnamon
- ¼ tsp of Nutmeg
- 2/3 cup of Erythritol Sweetener (e.g. Swerve)
- 6 large eggs
- ½ cup of Butter, melted
- 1 tsp of Vanilla
- ½ cup of Almond flour
- ¼ cup of diced pecans (optional)
- 1 pinch of salt
- 2 tbsp of softened Butter

Preparation Instructions:

1. Heat the oven to 350° F.
2. Use a non-stick spray to spray a donut pan.
3. Preparing the donuts:
4. Whisk the coconut flour, almond flour, flax meal, sweetener, baking powder, salt, nutmeg, and cinnamon together inside a medium bowl. Set aside.
5. Whisk the eggs, vanilla, and melted butter until it appears. Add all the dry ingredients into wet ingredients and mix.
6. Spoon the batter into the donut space and fill it ¾ of the way full.
7. Preparing the crumb topping:
8. Stir together the sweetener, almond meal, and salt inside a small bowl. Add the butter and mix. Thoroughly mix until all of the flour is well combined and the mixture is moistened throughout.
9. Topping the donuts:
10. Garnish the topping on the donuts, with fingers to break up the mixture until it is well mixed.
11. Place in the oven for 12-15 minutes or until the sides appear light brown.

Macros: Calories: 138g | Fat: 12g | Carbs: 3g | Fiber: 2g | Protein: 4g

47. Sopapilla Cheesecake Bars

Preparation time: 15 minutes
Cook time: 50 minutes
Servings: 16

Ingredients:

Dough Ingredients:

- 8 oz. Mozzarella cubed or shredded
- 2 oz. of Cream Cheese
- 1 large egg
- 1/3 cup of Almond flour
- 1/3 cup Coconut flour
- 2 tbsp of sweetener
- 1 tsp of Vanilla extract
- 1 tsp of baking powder

Cheesecake Filling Ingredients:

- 14 oz. of Cream Cheese
- 2 large eggs
- ½ cup of sweetener
- 1 tsp of vanilla

Cinnamon Topping:

- 2 tbsp. of sweetener or my sweetener
- 1 tbsp. of Cinnamon
- 2 tbsp. of melted Butter

Preparation Instructions:

1. Heat the oven to 350 ° F.
2. Place the cheese in a microwave for a minute. Stir, then microwave again for 30 seconds. Stir. Microwave again for another 30 seconds so that it becomes gloopy and uniform (at this point, it should appear like a fondue).
3. Add the rest of the cheese and the dough ingredients to a food processor. Press ½ of it into an eight-by-eight baking dish as soon as it is a uniform color. Press out the second half into an eight-by-eight square onto the top of a parchment paper.
4. Add the sweetener, eggs, and cream cheese in a food processor to make the cheesecake filling. Mix until smooth.
5. Pour the batter of cheesecake onto the bottommost layer of dough. Carefully put the rest of the square of dough on top and remove the parchment paper. Drizzle the cinnamon and sweetener on top and sprinkle with the melted butter.
6. Place in the oven for about 50-60 minutes until it appears golden brown.

48. Keto Espresso Chocolate Cheesecake Bars

Preparation time: 10 minutes
Cook time: 35 minutes
Servings: 16

Ingredients:

Chocolate Crust Ingredients:

- 7 tbsp. of melted Butter
- 2 cups of ultrafine, blanched Almond flour
- 3 tbsp. of Cocoa powder
- 1/3 cup granulated Erythritol sweetener

Cheesecake Ingredients:

- 16 oz. of full fat Cream Cheese
- 2 large eggs
- ½ cup of granulated Erythritol sweetener
- 2 tbsp. of instant Espresso powder
- 1 tsp. of Vanilla extract
- Extra cocoa powder for dusting over the top.

Preparation Instructions:

Preparation of the Chocolate Crust:

1. Heat the oven to 350° F.
2. Combine the almond flour, melted butter, cocoa powder and sweetener in a medium sized bowl.
3. Transfer the crust dough to a 9 x 9" pan coated with foil or parchment paper.
4. Firmly press the crust to the bottom of the pan.
5. Place the crust in the oven and bake for about 8 minutes.
6. Take out of the oven and set aside to cool.

Preparing the cheesecake filling:

1. Place the eggs, cream cheese, espresso powder, vanilla extract, and sweetener inside a blender and blend the mixture until smooth.
2. Pour over the crust and evenly spread out in the pan.
3. Bake for 25 minutes. Take out of the oven and allow it to cool. Dust it with the cocoa powder
4. Place in the refrigerator to chill. Afterwards, cut into four rows of squares to serve.

Macros: Calories: 232 Cal | Fat: 21g | Carbs: 5g | Fiber: 1.5g |Protein: 6g

49. Mini No-Bake Lemon Cheesecakes

Preparation time: 20 minutes
Cook time: —
Servings: 6

Ingredients:

Crust Ingredients:

- ½ cup of blanched Almond flour
- 2 tbsp. of powdered Erythritol-based Sweetener
- ⅛ tsp. of salt
- 2 tbsp. unsalted and melted Butter

Filling:

- 1 tbs. plus ¼ cup powdered Erythritol-based Sweetener
- ¾ cup (6 oz.) of softened Cream Cheese
- ¼ cup of heavy whipping cream kept at room temp
- ½ tsp. of Lemon extract
- 2 tsp. of grated Lemon Zest
- 2 tbsp. of fresh Lemon juice

Preparation Instructions:

Preparing the Crust Ingredients:

1. Line muffin pan with parchment paper or silicone.
2. Whisk the sweetener, almond flour. Add the melted butter and stir until mixture starts clumping together.
3. Place the crust in the muffin cups you've prepared and make sure to firmly press into the bottoms.

Preparing the Filling:

1. With an electric mixer, beat the cream cheese in a medium bowl. Add the sweetener until it is well combined.
2. Beat in the lemon extract, lemon juice, lemon zest, and the cream until smooth.
3. Share the filling mixture into the muffin cups you prepared and fill all of the cups to almost the top. Also, smoothen the top. In order to let go of air bubbles firmly tap the pan on a counter.
4. For 2 hours, place the pan in the fridge so that the filling becomes firm. Carefully remove the silicone layers or the parchment paper liners. Serve when ready.

Macros: Fat: 20.1g | Carbs: 3.9g | Protein: 4g | Erythritol: 17.5g | Fiber: 1.1g | Calories: 223

50. Chocolate Coconut Donuts

Preparation time: 10 minutes
Cook time: 13 minutes
Servings: 14

Ingredients:
- Chocolate Coconut Donuts
- 6 eggs at room temp
- ½ cup of Coconut flour
- 1/2 cup paleo or keto sweetener
- ¼ cup of Cocoa powder
- ¼ cup of Coconut oil melted or softened
- ¼ cup of Coconut Butter melted or softened
- ½ tsp. of Vanilla extract
- ½ tsp. of Coconut extract
- ½ tsp. of baking powder
- ½ tsp. of baking soda
- ¾ cup of paleo chocolate chips
- Chocolate Drizzle + Coconut Butter Glaze
- ½ cup of coconut melted butter
- 4 drops of liquid Vanilla stevia (optional)
- ¼ cup of melted Lily's chocolate chips placed on a double boiler
- 1tsp. of coconut oil
- 3 tbsp. of shredded and unsweetened coconut for garnish

Preparation Instructions:
1. Preparation of the chocolate coconut donuts:
2. Heat oven to 350 F and grease a donut pan.
3. Place the coconut flour, eggs, sweetener, coconut oil, cocoa powder, and coconut butter in a bowl and mix until smooth.
4. Mix in coconut extract and vanilla, baking soda, baking powder. Fold in the chocolate chips.
5. Place the donut batter into a gallon-size bag with a ½" hole space in a corner. Place the donut batter into greased donut pan, and fill each to about half.
6. Place in the oven for 12-13 minutes.
7. Take out immediately and place on a cooling rack.
8. Preparing the Coconut Butter Glaze + Chocolate Drizzle:
9. Place coconut butter inside a bowl that is a little bit bigger in diameter than donuts. Whisk in some drops of liquid vanilla stevia if you want.
10. Dip the top of the donut inside the coconut butter that is melted if you want, gently tapping or shaking to remove the excess.
11. Sprinkle shredded, unsweetened coconut on donut before the glaze sets.
12. Melt 1 tsp. of coconut oil and Lily's chocolate chips over a double boiler.
13. Sprinkle or drop the chocolate on the donut.

51. Low-carb Lemon Blueberry Donuts

Preparation time: 22 minutes
Cook time: _____
Servings: 8
Ingredients:
- 1/2 cup coconut flour
- Sweetener equivalent to 1/2 cup sugar
- 2 tsp. of baking powder
- 2 tsp. of Lemon zest
- ¼ tsp. of salt
- 4 large eggs
- ¼ cup of melted Butter (or Avocado oil)
- ¼ cup of freshly squeezed Lemon juice
- ¼ cup of Water
- ½ tsp. of Vanilla extract
- ½ tsp. of Lemon extract
- ½ cup of fresh Blueberries

Preparation Instructions:
1. Heat the oven to 325 F and grease a donut pan well.
2. Add the sweetener, coconut flour, lemon zest, baking powder, and salt in a large bowl. Stir in the eggs, lemon juice, oil, extracts, and water until it is well mixed. Carefully fold in the blueberries.
3. Fill the donut space to about ¾ full of batter and place in the oven for 18-22 minutes, until it is firm to the touch.

Macros: Fat: 10.22g | Calories: 91 | Carbohydrate: 6.32g | Protein: 4.22g | Fiber: 2.84g

52. Low-Carb Raspberry Lemon Loaf

Preparation time: 1 Hour 30 minutes
Cook time: ___
Servings: 10
Ingredients:
Preparing the Loaf:
- 3 large eggs
- 1 large egg white
- Zest and juice from 1 Lemon
- ¼ cup of melted Butter, virgin Coconut oil or Ghee
- 1 ½ cups of Almond flour
- 3/4 cup of powdered Swerve
- ¼ tsp of Sea salt
- 1 tsp of baking powder
- 1 cup of fresh Raspberries

Glaze & Topping Ingredients:
- ½ cup of powdered Swerve
- Zest and juice from 1 lemon
- ½ cup of fresh raspberries

Preparation Instructions:
1. Heat the oven to 350 °F and line a loaf pan with parchment paper.
2. Whisk together the dry cake ingredients in a large bowl. Beat the eggs with a hand mixer in another bowl.
3. Combine the melted butter (or ghee), lemon zest, and lemon juice. Mix in all of the dry ingredients.
4. Carefully fold in raspberries and combine with a spatula.
5. Transfer into the loaf pan and evenly spread with a spatula.
6. Bake for 1 hour or until a toothpick dipped into the middle comes out clean. When it has cooked through, take out from the oven, set aside and allow it to cool after which you add the glaze.
7. For the glaze, combine all the ingredients together inside a small bowl and thoroughly mix until it is well combined.
8. Pour over the cooled loaf. Garnish with raspberries.

Macros: Carbs 4.3 g | Protein 5.8 g | Fat 14.1 g | Calories 169 kcal

53. Gluten Free Chocolate Iced Coconut Donuts

Preparation time: 10 minutes
Cook time: 20 minutes
Servings: 8

Ingredients:

Donut Ingredients:

- ½ cup of Coconut flour
- ¼ cup of shredded unsweetened Coconut
- ¼ cup of Erythritol or low-carb sugar substitute
- ¼ tsp. of Stevia concentrated powder
- ¼ tsp. of Sea salt
- ¼ tsp. of baking soda
- 6 large eggs
- ½ cup of melted Coconut oil
- ¼ cup unsweetened almond milk
- 1 tbsp. of Vanilla extract

Icing Ingredients:

- ¼ cup of softened Butter
- 6 tbsp. of unsweetened Cocoa powder
- ¼ cup of powdered Erythritol or Swerve
- ¼ tbsp. of Stevia concentrated powder
- ¼ cup of unsweetened Almond milk
- ½ tbsp. of Vanilla extract

Preparation Instructions:

Preparing the Donuts:

1. Combine coconut, coconut flour, erythritol, salt, stevia and baking soda.
2. Add the eggs, almond milk, vanilla extract, coconut oil until well mixed.
3. Fill in the donut molds 2/3 full of batter.
4. Bake at 350 F for 20 minutes or until toothpick comes out clean.

Preparing the Icing:

1. Beat butter with erythritol, stevia and cocoa.
2. Mix in almond milk and vanilla extract. Beat until well blended.
3. Spread evenly over donuts.

Macros: Calories: 186kcal | Carbohydrates: 8g | Protein: 7g | Fat: 22g | Fiber: 5g

54. Lemon Zucchini Loaf

Preparation time: 1 Hour
Cook time: ____
Servings: 12

Ingredients:

Loaf Ingredients:

- 2 cups Almond flour
- 2 tsp. of baking powder
- ½ tsp. of Xanthan gum
- 1/4 tsp. of salt
- ½ cup of melted coconut oil
- 3/4 cup of granular Swerve
- 3 large eggs
- 1 tsp. of Vanilla extract
- 2 tbsp. of fresh Lemon juice
- 1 tbsp. of Lemon zest
- 1 cup of drained and shredded Zucchini

Glaze Ingredients:

- 1/3 cup of Swerve confectioners
- 2 tbsp. of lemon juice

Preparation Instructions:

1. Heat the oven to 325 F. Line a loaf pan with parchment paper.
2. Mix the baking powder, xanthan gum, and salt. Set aside.
3. Whisk together eggs, vanilla, oil, Swerve granular, and lemon juice in a separate mixing bowl.
4. Fold in the dry ingredients with the wet. Fold the zucchini and lemon zest into the batter.
5. Transfer to the loaf pan and place in the oven for about 50 minutes. When there is too much browning at the end of the bake time, cover with foil. A toothpick inserted at the center will usually come out clean if it has been well cooked. Place on a wire rack to allow it to cool down.
6. Whisk together lemon juice and Swerve confectioners. Sprinkle loaf with glaze and serve

Macros: Calories: 143g | Carbs: 2g | Fiber: 1g | Fat: 13g | Protein: 2g

OTHERS

55. Dairy-free Keto eggnog Rocket Fuel Latte
Preparation time: 5 minutes
Total time: 5 minutes
Servings: 1
Ingredients:
- ¼ cup of Coconut Milk, full-fat
- 1 cup (8.5 oz.) of brewed Coffee
- 1-2 egg yolks
- 1 tbsp. of Coconut oil or MCT oil
- ⅛ tsp. of ground Allspice
- 2 tbsp. of grass-fed collagen
- ¼ tsp. of ground Cinnamon
- 2-3 drops of liquid Stevia, alcohol-free
- ⅛ tsp. of ground Nutmeg

Preparation Instructions:
Add all ingredients to a blender and blend for a minute. Garnish with cinnamon.

56. Pumpkin Spice Rocket Fuel Lattes
Preparation time: 5 minutes
Cook time: 1 minutes
Total time: 6 minutes
Servings: 1
Ingredients:
- 2 tbsp. of Coconut Milk, full-fat
- 1 ½ tsp. of Pumpkin Pie spice
- ¼ tsp. of vanilla extract, alcohol-free
- 2-4 drops of liquid Stevia, alcohol-free
- 1 tbsp. of Pumpkin Puree
- 1-2 tbsp. of Coconut oil or MCT oil
- 1 cup (8.5 oz.) of brewed coffee

Preparation Instructions:
Add all ingredients to a blender and blend for a minute. Garnish with cinnamon.

57. Keto White Chocolate Rocket Fuel Latte
Preparation time: 5 minutes
Total time: 5 minutes
Serves: 1
Ingredients:
- 8 oz. of favorite tea or coffee
- 1 tbsp. of Coconut oil or powdered MCT oil or liquid MCT oil
- 1 tbsp. of Cacao Butter
- 1 tbsp. of Hemp Hearts or preferred seed/nut butter
- 2-4 drops Stevia, alcohol-free
- 1 tbsp. of grass-fed Collagen

Preparation Instructions:
Add all ingredients to a blender and blend for a minute. Enjoy!

58. Pumpkin Caramel Latte

Preparation time: 3 minutes
Cook time: 5 minutes
Total time: 8 minutes
Servings: 1
Ingredients:
Pumpkin Latte Ingredients:
- 1 cup Almond milk, unsweetened
- 2 tbsp. of unsweetened Pumpkin Puree
- 1 tbsp. of sweetener of choice
- ½ tsp. of Pumpkin Pie spice
- ¼ tsp. of Vanilla extract
- ¼ cup of strong brewed coffee or hot Espresso

Caramel Sauce Ingredients:
- ½ tbsp of butter
- ½ tbsp of coconut milk or heavy cream
- 1 tsp of sweetener of choice
- ⅛ tsp of molasses

Toppings:
- 2 tbsp. of whipped coconut cream or whipped cream
- A pinch of cinnamon

Preparation Instructions:
1. Mix the caramel ingredients over medium heat in a small pan until completely melted, bubbling and combined. Take out from heat and allow it to thicken and let it aside.
2. Mix pumpkin pie spice, vanilla extract, sweetener of choice, pumpkin puree and almond milk and heat the mixture.
3. Remove from heat and beat until it becomes frothy.
4. Pour the ¼ of the coffee or espresso in a tall coffee cup.
5. Put the pumpkin latte mixture on the top of the hot espresso or coffee.
6. Top using the whipped coconut cream or whipped cream.
7. Sprinkle with a pinch of cinnamon on top and with caramel sauce.

59. Coconut Almond Mocha

Preparation time: 1 minutes
Cook time: 3 minutes
Total time: 4 minutes
Servings: 1
Ingredients:
- ½ of cup brewed coffee
- 2/3 cup coconut milk or almond milk, unsweetened
- 2 tsp. of cacao or cocoa powder for paleo do not use this if you are using unsweetened chocolate almond milk.
- 1 tbsp of coconut butter or use 1/8 tsp of coconut extract
- 1/8 tsp of GF almond extract (optional though)
- Any sweetener of choice

Preparation Instructions:
1. In a small saucepan, add all the ingredients and allow to heat over a medium heat. Stir and warm using a whisk and do not stop until all the ingredients inside have been combined and melted.
2. Continue heating to the temperature of choice.

60. Vanilla Latte Martini

Preparation time: 20 minutes
Total time: 20 minutes
Servings: 2 servings
Ingredients:
- 1 tbsp of Cream
- 2 oz. of Vanilla Vodka
- 1½ oz. of homemade Coffee Liqueur

Preparation Instructions:
Add ice to cocktail shaker. Pour in cream, vanilla vodka, and coffee liqueur. Thoroughly shake and pour into 2 cold martini glasses.

61. Low-carb Peppermint Hot Chocolate

Preparation time: 30 minutes
Servings: 4
Ingredients:
- 1/3 cup Cocoa powder.
- ½ cup of Almond milk (or 2 cans of coconut milk).
- ¾ oz. of dark Chocolate
- 1 ½ tsp. of Peppermint extract (optional).
- ¾ cup of Sweetener

Preparation Instructions:
1. Over medium to low heat, heat the coconut milk.
2. Whisk the cocoa powder until no lumps appear.
3. Add the sweetener and chocolate and keep stirring.
4. Melt the chocolate. Add the peppermint extract and keep stirring to mix very well.

62. Keto Cappuccino

Preparation time: 2 minutes
Total time: 2 minutes
Servings: 1
Ingredients:
- ¼ cup of almond milk, unsweetened (or hemp milk)
- Few drops liquid stevia, vanilla or chocolate
- Strong brewed coffee (or 1 shot espresso)

Preparation Instructions:
Over medium heat, heat the almond milk. Prepare a shot of decaf espresso and pour it into a cup. Pour in the almond milk and top with foam. Add the stevia and stir.

63. Sugar-Free Coffee Liqueur

Preparation time: 5 minutes
Cook time: 15 minutes
Total time: 20 minutes
Servings: 20

Ingredients:

Coffee Liqueur Preparation

- 3/4 cup of Swerve Sweetener
- 2 cups of water
- 1/8 tsp of monk fruit extract
- ¼ cup of ground coffee
- 1 ½ cup of vodka
- 1 tsp of vanilla extract
- 1 tbsp of cocoa powder

Mexican Coffee Preparation:

- 1 oz. of coffee liqueur
- 1 cup freshly brewed coffee
- ½ oz. of tequila if you're feeling bold or add a touch more vodka or coffee liqueur
- Sprinkle of cinnamon
- 2 tbsp. whipped cream

Preparation Instructions:

1. Mix coffee grounds, monk fruit extracts, erythritol and water in a medium saucepan and heat over medium to high heat.
2. Allow to boil and then reduce the heat and let simmer for ten minutes. Allow it to cool.
3. Pour mixture into a jar and include vanilla extract, cocoa powder, and vodka.
4. Close the glass jar and keep it a cool dark spot and let it cool. Wait for a minimum of 3 weeks and make sure you keep shaking every couple of days.
5. Run the mixture over a fine sieve. Then run over a coffee filter again.
6. Mix coffee and tequila in a big coffee mug for the Mexican Coffee. You can top with cinnamon and whipped cream

64. Low-carb Gingerbread Lattes

Preparation time: 5 minutes
Cook time:10 minutes
Total time: 15 minutes
Servings: 2

Ingredients:

- ¼ cup organic heavy whipping Cream
- 1 cup unsweetened organic Almond Milk
- ½-1 tsp of ground Ginger
- ¼ tsp of ground Cinnamon
- ¼ tsp of Vanilla extract
- ½ strongly brewed Coffee or 2 shots of Espresso
- 2 or more packets Organic Stevia

Preparation Instructions:

1. Add the cinnamon, ginger, cream, and almond milk in a medium saucepan and place over medium heat. Allow to simmer and decrease the heat and allow it to cook for about 5 minutes.
2. Remove from heat and add vanilla extract and stir. Sieve by passing through a fine mesh and compress the solid to extract more flavor from them.
3. With a whisk, froth the creamer and pour into two coffee mugs. Sweeten with organic stevia and add the coffee.

65. Keto Hot Buttered Rum Mix

Preparation time: 10 minutes
Total time: 10 minutes
Servings: 4.5 Cups

Ingredients:

- 1 cup of Butter
- 1 cup of granulated Swerve
- 3 tbsp. of sugar free maple syrup
- 1 tsp of Vanilla extract
- 1 cup of heavy Cream
- 1 ½ cup powdered Swerve
- ¼ tsp. of ground Nutmeg
- 1/8 tsp. of ground Cloves
- ¼ tsp. of ground Cinnamon

Preparation Instructions:

1. Preparing the Mix
2. With a hand mixing device on a medium speed, mix the vanilla, maple syrup, granulated swerve, and cream together with the butter in a large mixing bowl for 3 minutes. Stop mixing when the mixture appears fluffy and light.
3. Add the clove, cinnamon, nutmeg, powdered swerve, and heavy cream and allow to mix on low speed and continue mixing until the mixture becomes smooth.
4. Preparing the Drink
5. Mix 1-2 oz. of spiced rum in half cup of water and include 2-3 tbsp. of keto buttered rum batter.

66. Pumpkin Pie Martini

Preparation time: 10 minutes
Total time: 10 minutes
Servings: 2

Ingredients:

For the Rim:

- 2 tbsp. of finely ground pecans
- ¼ tsp of ground Cinnamon
- ½ tbsp. of granulated Erythritol or Swerve Sweetener

For the Martini:

- 2 oz. of Vanilla Vodka
- 1½ oz. of dark Rum
- 2 tbsp. of Pumpkin Puree
- 2 tbsp. of heavy Cream
- 1 tbsp of Swerve Sweetener or granulated Erythritol
- ¼ tsp of ground Cinnamon
- 1/8 tsp of ground Ginger
- Pinch of freshly grated Nutmeg

Preparation Instructions:

1. Place cinnamon, swerve, and ground pecans on a shallow plate. Wet the borders of 2 martini glasses and place inside pecan mixture. Set aside.
2. Put ice in a large cocktail shaker and add ginger, cinnamon, swerve, cream, pumpkin, rum, and vodka.
3. Thoroughly mix the mixture by shaking it. Strain the mixture into a made martini glass.
4. Sprinkle with a pinch of nutmeg and serve.

67. Peppermint Hot Chocolate Mix

Preparation: Time 5 minutes
Total Tim: 5 minutes
Servings: 4

Ingredients:

- 3 tsp. of Stevia extract powder
- 1 cup of Cocoa powder
- 1 1/2 tsp Sea salt
- 1 cup coconut Milk powder
- 6 tbsp. Collagen Hydrolysate Gelatin powder
- 1 1/4 tsp Vanilla Bean powder
- 12 drops Peppermint Essential Oil

Preparation Instructions:

1. With the exception of essential oil, sift all the ingredients into a large bowl.
2. Thoroughly mix. Add the essential oil and mix again.
3. Mix 3 tbsp. of cocoa powder, and one cup of hot water.

68. Keto Brown Butter Pralines

Preparation time: 5 minutes
Cook time: 11 minutes
Servings: 10

Ingredients:

- 2 sticks of butter, salted
- 2/3 Cup of Heavy Cream
- 2/3 Cup of 1:1 sugar free sweetener
- ½ tsp. of Xanthan gum
- 2 cups of chopped Pecans
- sea salt

Preparation Instructions:

1. Line a cookie sheet with a silicone baking mat or parchment paper.
2. Brown the butter inside a saucepan over medium high heat, stirring frequently. Stir in the heavy cream, sweetener, and xanthan gum. Remove from heat.
3. Add the nuts and stir, and refrigerate for about 1 hour, stirring occasionally. This will make the mixture get really thick. Scoop into 10 cookie shapes onto the baking sheets and drizzle with the salt. Refrigerate on baking sheet until hardened.

69. Keto Chocolate Chip Cookies

Preparation time: 10 minutes
Cook time: 12 minutes
Servings: 21
Ingredients:
- ¾ cup of coconut oil or Softened butter
- 2/3 cup of Swerve Sweetener
- 2 large eggs
- 2 tsp of Vanilla Extract
- 2 cups of Almond Flour
- ½ tsp of baking soda
- ½ tsp of salt
- ½ 9-oz. Lily's Chocolate Chips Bag

Preparation Instructions:
1. Heat the oven to 350 F.
2. Include coconut oil (or softened butter) and swerve sweetener inside a hand mixer (or stand mixer with a large bowl), combine on medium heat until combined.
3. Include vanilla and 2 eggs and mix well.
4. Combine baking soda, salt, and almond flour in a medium bowl.
5. Add dry ingredients to wet ingredients and make sure to mix the mixture until combined.
6. Carefully fold inside Lily's Chocolate Chips.
7. Scoop about 18 to 21 cookies onto coated baking sheet. Flatten them by using hands to press down on the top slightly.
8. Place in the oven for about 10-12 minutes
9. Allow it cool on cookie sheets for 30 minutes.
Macros: Servings: 1g | Calories: 179kcal | Carbohydrates: 4g | Protein: 5g | Fat: 17g | Fiber: 2g

70. Sugar Free Chocolate Pie

Preparation time: 4 Hours
Cook time: 15 minutes
Servings: 8
Ingredients:
- 1 cup of Almond Flour Pie Crust
- 1 cup of Swerve Sweetener
- 1 tbsp. of Corn starch
- 2 tsp. of Xanthan gum
- ¼ tsp salt
- 3 egg yolks
- 1 tsp. of Vanilla extract
- 2 ½ cups of Unsweetened Almond Milk
- 3 tbsp. of Cocoa Powder
- 6 pieces of chopped Unsweetened baker's chocolate
- 2 tbsp. of Butter

Preparation Instructions:
1. Prepare the pie crust and set aside to cool.
2. In a medium saucepan, add the cornstarch, Swerve, xanthan gum, and salt and whisk to combine. Add the vanilla, almond milk, and egg yolks, cocoa powder, and continue whisking. Place over medium heat.
3. Remove from heat when the mixture is thick like pudding and starts to bubble. Stir in butter and the chopped chocolate until thoroughly melted.
4. Transfer the chocolate pudding into the pie crust and let set up in the refrigerator for at least 4 hours.
5. Slice and serve with whipped cream
Macros: Calories: 424kcal | Carbohydrates: 13g | Fat: 38g | Saturated Fat: 12g | Fiber: 8g

71. Low-carb Blueberry Crisp

Preparation time: 5 minutes
Cook time: 20 minutes
Servings: 2

Ingredients:

- 1 cup Blueberries fresh or frozen
- ¼ cup of Pecan halves
- 1/8 cup of Almond Meal/flour
- 2 tbsp. of Butter
- 2 tbsp. of Swerve sweetener divided
- 1 tbsp. of Ground flax
- ½ tsp. of Cinnamon
- ½ tsp. of Vanilla extract
- ¼ tsp. of Kosher salt
- 2 tbsp. of heavy cream

Preparation Instructions:

1. Heat the oven to 400 F.
2. Add 1/2 tbsp. of swerve sweetener and 1/2 cup of blueberries in ramekins. Mix very well.
3. In a food processor, add almond flour, pecans, 1 tbsp. of swerve sweetener, butter, kosher salt, vanilla, cinnamon, ground flax and. Mix until the ingredients are combined.
4. Evenly spread the mixture on the top of the blueberries. Position the ramekins on the top a baking sheet and place in the center of the oven for 15-20 minutes to bake or until the topping ingredients appears toasty brown.
5. Serve with a tbsp. of heavy cream sprinkled over top of each.

Macros: l/ 6g protein/ 17g carbs/ 6g fiber/ 35g fat

72. Sugar Free Chocolate Bark with Bacon and Almonds

Preparation time: 30 minutes
Servings: 8

Ingredients:

- 19-oz. bag of Lily's Dark Chocolate Chips
- ½ cup of chopped Almonds
- 2 slices of Bacon crumbled and cooked

Preparation Instructions:

1. Set the microwave on high and microwave the chocolate chips for 30 seconds in a microwave safe bowl and stir. Microwave it for another 15 seconds and then stir one more time.
2. Add the chopped almonds into the melted chocolate and pour onto a baking sheet coated with parchment paper in a thin layer of about ½ inch.
3. Sprinkle the bacon onto the chocolate and use a spatula to press.
4. Refrigerate for 20 minutes so that the chocolate gets completely hardened.
5. Remove the parchment paper from the chocolate and cut into eight pieces.

Macros: For 1/8 of recipe: 157 Cal / 12.8g fat / 12.7g carbs / 7.5g fiber / 4g protein

73. Keto Donuts

Preparation time: 10 minutes
Cook time: 15 minutes
Servings: 12

Ingredients:

- 2 large eggs at room temp
- ¼ cup of unsweetened Almond milk
- ¼ tsp. of Apple Cider Vinegar
- 1 tsp. of Vanilla extract
- 2 tbsp. of melted Butter, or Ghee
- ¼ cup of granulated Monk fruit sweetener
- 1 cup of fine blanched Almond flour
- ½ tbsp. of Coconut flour
- ¼ tsp. of Xanthan gum
- 1 tsp. of ground Cinnamon
- 1 ½ tsp. of baking powder
- ½ tsp. of baking soda
- 1/8 tsp. of fine Sea salt

Cinnamon Sugar Coating Ingredients:

- ¼ cup of granulated Monk fruit, granulated Erythritol or Swerve
- 1 tsp. of ground Cinnamon
- 1 1/2 tbsp. of melted butter, ghee or even paleo

Chocolate Glaze Ingredients:

- 2 oz. of melted No sugar dark chocolate
- 1 tsp. of melted Coconut oil
- 1 tsp. of powdered Monk fruit sweetener

Preparation Instructions:

1. Mix the almond milk, eggs, apple cider vinegar vanilla, melted ghee, and monk fruit sweetener in a large bowl. Whisk until smooth and well mixed.
2. Combine coconut flour, almond flour, xanthan gum, baking powder, cinnamon, salt and baking soda in a separate medium bowl. Slowly add the dry ingredients to the wet ingredients. Mix well.
3. Pour into a greased 12 space silicone donut pan.
4. Place in an oven heated to 350 F for 21-24 minutes until it appears golden brown.
5. Take out the pan from the oven and set aside so that the donuts become cool enough to be touched.

Cinnamon Coating Preparation:

1. As the donuts are in the oven baking, stir together the cinnamon and granulated sweetener in a small bowl.
2. Melt the butter or ghee in a separate bowl.
3. Dunk each cooled donuts into the melted ghee and then roll into the sweetener cinnamon coating.

Chocolate Glaze Preparation:

Place the coconut oil and chopped chocolate in a small heat-safe bowl and place in a microwave to melt it. Stir in the sweetener until it is well mixed.

74. Healthy Peanut Butter Balls

Preparation time: 20 minutes
Cook time: _____
Servings: 8

Ingredients:

- 1 cup of finely chopped salted Peanuts
- 1 cup of peanut Butter
- 1 cup of powdered Sweetener like swerve
- 8 oz. of sugarless chocolate chips

Preparation Instructions:

1. Mix the peanut butter, sweetener, and chopped peanuts together. Divide the dough into about 18 pieces and make into balls. Place on a baking sheet lined with wax paper. Refrigerate.
2. Melt the chocolate chips in a double boiler or microwave.
3. Dip the peanut butter balls into the chocolate provided and place them back on the wax paper.
4. Refrigerate until they set.

75. Keto Chocolate Peanut Butter Hearts

Preparation time: 5 minutes
Cook time: 5 minutes
Servings: 20

Ingredients:

- 2 cups of smooth Peanut Butter
- ¾ cup of sticky Sweetener
- 1 cup of Coconut flour
- 1 to 2 cups of Chocolate Chips

Preparation Instructions:

1. Line a large tray or plate using parchment paper. Set aside.
2. In a stovetop or microwave-safe bowl, add peanut butter with sticky sweetener and keep melting it until becomes combined.
3. Add the coconut flour and thoroughly combine. Add more coconut flour if the batter is too thin. Let it sit for 10 minutes to allow it to thicken.
4. Form about 18 to 20 small balls of peanut butter dough. Flatten each of the balls and cut with a heart-shaped cookie cutter. Remove the excess peanut butter dough from the sides. Refrigerate.
5. Melt the chocolate chips. With two forks, dip each of the peanut butter heart into the chocolate so that it becomes uniformly coated. Refrigerate until it becomes firm.

Macros: Calories: 95 kCal | Carbs: 7g | Protein: 5g | Fat: 6g | Fiber: 5g

76. White Chocolate Peanut Butter Blondies

Preparation time: 10 minutes
Cook time: 25 minutes
Servings: 16
Ingredients:

- ½ cup of peanut butter
- 4 tbsp. of softened butter
- 2 eggs
- 1 tsp of Vanilla
- 3 tbsp of melted cocoa butter
- ¼ cup of Almond flour
- 1 tbsp of Coconut flour
- ½ cup of sweetener
- ¼ cup of chopped cocoa butter

Preparation Instructions:

1. Heat the oven to 350 F. Spray the bottom of a 9 x 9 baking dish with cooking spray.
2. Mix the first 5 ingredients until they become smooth. Add the chopped cocoa butter, sweetener, and flours. Spread in the baking dish that you prepared.
3. Bake for 25 minutes until the middle stop being jiggle and the sides appear golden.
4. Completely cool and then place in the refrigerator to chill for at least 2 to 3 hours before cutting.

77. Keto Texas Sheet Cake with Chocolate Avocado Frosting

Preparation time:15
Cook time: 30
Servings: 4-8
Ingredients:

Texas Sheet Cake

- 1/2 cup coconut oil, melted
- 1/2 cup cold-brewed coffee (recipe here)
- 3 tbsp. cacao powder
- 1/2 tsp cinnamon
- 1 cup almond flour
- 1/2 cup coconut flour
- 1 tsp of baking soda
- 1/4 cup liquid monk fruit extract
- 1 tsp vanilla extract
- "Buttermilk" (1/2 cup almond milk + 1 1/2 tbsp. apple cider vinegar)
- 2 eggs

Chocolate Avocado Frosting

- 1/2 large avocado (3 tbsp.)
- 2 tbsp. cacao powder
- 1 tbsp coconut oil
- 1/4 cup unsweetened lite coconut milk (or dilute 1/8 cup full-fat coconut milk with 1/8 cup water)
- 2 tsp. liquid monk fruit extract

Preparation Instructions

1. Preheat the oven to 400 F.
2. In a small mixing bowl, combine coconut oil, cold brew, cacao powder, and cinnamon.
3. In a large mixing bowl, combine the almond flour, coconut flour, baking soda, and monk fruit extract.
4. In another mixing bowl, whisk together the "buttermilk" (almond milk + apple cider vinegar), eggs, and vanilla extract, then add it to the mixture.
5. Mix completely.
6. Pour batter into a 9×13 dish and bake for 20 minutes.
7. Combine all frosting ingredients together and mix until completely smooth.
8. Once the cake is completely cooled, spread the frosting, then cut into slices.

78. Keto Lemon Bars

Preparation time: 10 minutes
Cook time: 30 minutes
Servings:2-4

Ingredients:

- 1.5 cups blanched almond meal
- ½ cup softened butter or ghee
- Pinch of salt
- 1-2 tbsp xylitol or erythritol
- 1 cup blanched almond meal
- 1/4 - 1/3 cup xylitol or erythritol
- 1 cup lemon juice
- Zest of 3-4 lemons
- 4 eggs

Preparation Instructions

1. Preheat oven to 350 F. Mix the first 4 ingredients together to make the base. Press the mixture evenly into a 9x9 parchment paper-lined baking dish. Bake for 10-12 minutes or until golden brown.
2. In a large bowl, mix the remaining ingredients together for the filling.
3. Pour the filling onto the pre-baked, cooled crust and bake for 25 minutes.
4. Remove from the oven and cool down.
5. Cut the slice into 20 squares and enjoy.

Macros: (per square) Calories: 86, Fat: 7.1g, Saturated Fat: 0.9g, Cholesterol: 33mg, Salt: 12mg, Carbs: 3.1g, Fiber: 1.5g, Sugar: 0.6g, Protein: 3.6g

PASTRIES

79. Walnut Pinwheels or Rugelach Pastries

Preparation time: 20 minutes
Cook time: 10 minutes
Servings: 4

Ingredients

- 112 grams or 1 cup mozzarella cheese, part skim
- 56 grams or 4 tbsp. mascarpone cheese
- 28 grams or 2 tbsp. butter
- 50 grams or 1 large egg
- 4 grams or 1 tsp vanilla extract
- 64 grams or 1/2 cup almond flour
- 8 grams or 1 tbsp coconut flour
- 5 grams or 2 tsp. cinnamon
- 16 grams or 2 tbsp. chopped walnuts
- Optional - Sweetener of choice. Reserve 1 tsp for sprinkling in the center.

Preparation Instructions:

1.   Mix the mozzarella cheese, mascarpone cheese and butter in a microwave safe bowl. Microwave for 30 second intervals, stirring each time until the cheeses are completely melted.
2.   In a food processor fitted with the 'S' blade, mix the melted cheese, egg, vanilla extract, optional sweetener, almond flour and coconut flour. Blend this mixture together until completely smooth. Make sure you scrape the sides several times to incorporate all the ingredients evenly.
3.   Depending on preference and the temperature of the cheese, the dough can be very loose, with a texture like pancake batter. Scrape the dough into a bowl, cover with plastic wrap and refrigerate until it is cool.
4.   Place a large piece of plastic wrap on the counter and scrape the dough out of the bowl onto the plastic wrap. Cover with another piece of plastic wrap and roll the dough until it is about 1/4 inch thick. Remove the top piece of plastic wrap.
5.   Sprinkle the cinnamon, walnuts and additional sweetener evenly on the surface of the dough. Using the edge of the plastic wrap to assist, begin rolling the dough into a pinwheel shape. If you are making Rugelach, stop once the roll has reached 1 inch in diameter which is about half of the dough. Then cut the dough in half and start a second roll again. If you are making pinwheel shaped pastries, roll the entire batch into 1 roll, 2 inches in diameter.
6.   Keep the rolled dough on the bottom piece of plastic and carefully re-wrap. Place in the freezer for 2 hours or until it is frozen.
7.   Preheat the oven to 350 F. Line a cookie sheet with parchment paper. Cut the frozen dough into 1/4 inch slices for pinwheel pastries or into 1 inch sections for Rugelach and bake the pastries for 15-17 minutes or until lightly browned.

Macros: 7g Fat / 3g protein / 1g Net Carbs

80. Low-Carb Lemon Danish Pastries

Preparation time: 20
Cook time:30
Servings:6
Ingredients
For the pastry
- 2/3 cup almond flour
- 1/4 cup coconut flour
- 1/4 cup stevia/erythritol blend
- 1 1/4 tsp grain-free baking powder
- 1 large egg + 1 more for egg wash
- 1 1/2 cup part-skim mozzarella cheese, shredded
- 4 1/2 tbsp. butter
- 1 tbsp vanilla extract

For the Filling
- 8 oz. cream cheese, room temperature
- 3 tbsp. stevia/erythritol blend
- 1/2 tsp lemon extract
- zest of 1 lemon

Preparation Instructions

Preheat the oven to 350º F. Line a cookie sheet with parchment paper.

Preparation of the filling

Put the cream cheese, stevia erythritol mix, lemon extract and lemon zest to a medium mixing bowl. Using a mixer, combine ingredients at low speed. When added, turn mixer to high speed and blend until slightly fluffy.

Preparation of the pastry dough

1.   In a small mixing bowl, combine the almond flour, coconut flour, stevia/erythritol mix and baking powder using a whisk.
2.   Break one egg in a small bowl. Add vanilla extract and whisk briefly. Add this mixture to the dry ingredients and combine using a spoon. The mixture will appear mealy and egg will not mix in completely.
3.   Break the other egg in a small bowl and whisk briefly. Reserve for later.
4.   Melt mozzarella cheese and butter in a medium saucepan over low heat, stirring constantly.
5.   When melted, remove from heat and add dry ingredients to the cheese and butter, stirring vigorously. Place dough on a piece of parchment and knead with hands together until it resembles bread dough.
6.   Pat into a disk shape and cover with the other piece of parchment. Roll dough into a rectangular shape about 12" by 9". Remove top parchment.
7.   With a butter knife, gently cut the dough in half lengthwise, then into six equal pieces crosswise to make a total of 12 small rectangles.
8.   Spoon the filling over six of the rectangles, dividing it equally among the rectangles and keeping the filling about 1/2 inch from the edges.
9.   Carefully cover each of the rectangles with filling with a rectangle without filling. You might need to stretch it a bit to make it fit. Put the edges together and press edges with the tines of a fork. Place pastries on the prepared cookie sheet. Cut steam holes in the top of each pastry using the tip of a sharp knife.
10.   With a pastry brush, lightly brush a bit of the previously reserved egg over the top of the pastries. Place pastries in the bottom third of the preheated oven.
11.   Bake for 15-18 minutes or until golden brown color.

81. Low-carb Almond Pastry

Preparation time: 20
Cook time: 10
Servings:2

Ingredients

- 4 oz mozzarella
- 1 oz cream cheese
- 1 tbsp butter
- 1/2 cup almond flour
- 1 tbsp sweetener
- 1 tsp almond extract
- 1 egg
- *Topping Ingredients (optional)*
- 1 cup slivered almonds
- 2 tbsp butter softened
- 1/4 cup + 2 tbsp sweetener

Preparation Instructions

1. Start by preheating the oven to 350º F. Grease a small baking sheet.
2. Put cheese in a microwave-safe bowl. Microwave one minute. Stir. Microwave 30 seconds. Stir. At this point, all the cheese should be melted. Microwave 30 more seconds until uniform and gloopy (it should look like cheese fondue at this point).
3. Mix in the egg, almond extract, 1 tbsp sweetener, and almond flour. Once it is uniform, press it into the baking pan.
4. Mix the almonds, softened butter, and 1/4 cup sweetener. Spread this out on top of the dough.
5. Bake at 350 F for 30-35 minutes until you get a golden color. Remove from the oven and sprinkle it with the remaining 2 tbsp sweetener.
6. Cool for at least 10 min. Cut into squares and serve warm.

Macros: Total Fat 12g, Saturated Fat 4g, Cholesterol 31mg, Sodium 97mg, Potassium 78mg, Total Carbohydrates 3g, Dietary Fiber 1g, Sugars 0g, Protein 5g

82. Pecan Danish

Preparation time: 15 minutes
Cook time: 20 minutes
Servings: 10

Ingredients

- 8 oz mozzarella
- 2 oz cream cheese
- 1/3 cup almond flour
- 1/3 cup coconut flour
- 1/3 cup ground golden flax or additional almond flour
- 2 tbsp sweetener
- 1 egg
- 1 tsp of baking powder

Pecan Filling Ingredients:

- 3/4 cup pecans
- 1.5 tbsp softened butter
- 3 tbsp sweetener

Topping Ingredients (optional)

- 1/4 cup chopped pecans

Preparation Instructions

1. Preheat the oven to 350 F.
2. Put cheese in a microwave safe bowl and microwave for one minute. Stir and microwave 30 again for a few seconds. Stir and at this point, all the cheese should have been melted. Microwave 30 more seconds until uniform and gloopy (it should look like cheese fondue at this point). Alternatively, you can melt the cheese in a small saucepan over low heat.
3. Pour the rest of the dough ingredients and the cheese in a food processor. Mix using the dough blade until a uniform color. Once it is uniform, divide the dough into 12 pieces, and press them out into 12 circles on a parchment lined baking sheet.
4. Put the ingredients for the pecan butter in a food processor and process until smooth. Divide it into between the circles of dough. Fold up two edges of each circle. Then sprinkle with remaining chopped pecans.
5. Bake for 20-25 minutes or until golden brown.

Macros: Total Fat 16g Saturated Fat 4g Cholesterol 33mg Sodium 147mg Potassium 140mg Total Carbohydrates 5g Dietary Fiber 3g Sugars 1g Protein 7g

83. Glazed Crumb Keto Donuts

Preparation time: 30 minutes
Cook time: 35 minutes
Servings:6

Ingredients

For the Donuts:

- 2 tbsp butter softened
- 1/4 cup sour cream
- 2 tbsp sweetener
- 1/2 cup of equal parts almond flour, coconut flour, ground golden flax
- 1 egg
- 1 tsp vanilla
- 1/2 tsp of baking powder
- tiny pinch of salt

For the Crumb Topping:

- 1/2 cup almond flour
- 2 tsp coconut flour
- 3 tbsp butter softened
- 3 tbsp sweetener

Glaze:

- 2 tbsp butter
- 1/2 cup sweetener

Preparation Instructions

1. Preheat the oven to 350 F.
2. Mix all the ingredients for the batter. Divide them into 12 mini donut molds.
3. Mix the ingredients for the crumbs. They will be large moist crumbs. Spread on top of the donut batter.
4. Bake for 25 min. If the crumbs start to get too brown you can cover them with foil.
5. In a small saucepan over low heat melt the butter and sweetener. Cook on low, whisking occasionally, for 12-15 minutes until golden. Cool for at least 10 minutes. Keep whisking occasionally as it cools to avoid it separating.
6. Cool the donuts and put them on a wire rack. Put a clean rimmed baking sheet under them. Spoon glaze over donuts.
7. Then begin to scoop up the glaze that dripped off onto the baking sheet and spoon it on them again. Repeat. Doing this helps them get a nice thick coating.

Macros Total Fat 12g Saturated Fat 5g Cholesterol 33mg

Sodium 70mg Potassium 32mg Total Carbohydrates 2g

Dietary Fiber 1g Protein 2g

84. Gluten-Free Cinnamon Rolls

Preparation time: 30 minutes
Cook time: 40 minutes
Servings: 6

Ingredients

For the Dough:
- 8 oz shredded mozzarella (2 cups)
- 2 oz cream cheese
- 1 egg
- 1/3 cup almond flour
- 1/3 cup coconut flour
- 1/3 cup ground golden flax (or additional almond flour)
- 2 tsp sweetener
- 1 tsp vanilla
- 1 tbsp baking powder

For the Filling:
- 2 tbsp butter , softened
- 1/4 cup sweetener
- 1/2 tsp molasses (optional but this tiny amount adds negligible carbs and gives a nice flavor)
- 2 scoops Better Stevia using the included teeny tiny spoon (this comes to 90 mg of pure stevia if you are converting from another brand)
- 2 tsp cinnamon

Cream Cheese Icing:
- 3 oz cream cheese , softened
- 1 tbsp butter , softened
- 1/4 cup sweetener, finely ground
- 1 tsp vanilla

Preparation Instructions

1. Start by preheating the oven to 350 .
2. Then put the cheese in a microwave-safe bowl. Microwave it for one minute. Stir it. Microwave again 30 seconds. Stir again but at this point, all the cheese should have been melted. Microwave it for 30 more seconds until it is uniform and gloopy (note: it should look like cheese fondue at this point).
3. Mix in the egg, vanilla, 2 tsp sweetener, baking powder, flours, and flax. Or pulse in a food processor until thoroughly combined. If mixing by hand you may need to dump it onto wax paper and knead it by hand to thoroughly incorporate the ingredients.
4. Press it out into a 9×12 rectangle on parchment paper.
5. Mix together the 1/4 cup gentle sweet, stevia, cinnamon, and molasses. Spread the dough with 2 tbsp of butter and sprinkle with sweetener combo. Roll up along the long side. Slice into 3/4 inch thick slices. Put them in a greased baking dish or pie plate.
6. Put the cinnamon buns into the oven. Bake for 35-40 minutes until golden brown.
7. Meanwhile, make the icing. Mix the cream cheese, butter, sweetener, and vanilla with an electric mixer until smooth. Set aside.
8. Let the cinnamon buns cool for 5 min and spread the icing over the top. Serve warm.

Macros Total Fat 15g Saturated Fat 7g Cholesterol 49mg
Sodium 196mg Potassium 178mg Total Carbohydrates 5g
Dietary Fiber 3g Sugars 1g Protein 7g

85. Keto Sigara Boregi

Preparation time: 20 minutes
Cook time: 20 minutes
Servings: 4

Ingredients

- 1 QK Puff Pastry #3 (unsalted)
- 200g Greek Feta cheese (crumbled)
- ½ TBSP unsweetened almond or coconut milk
- a small handful of fresh mint or parsley leaves
- 2 small eggs - beaten in separate bowls
- ¼ tsp paprika
- a little sesame flour for dusting

Preparation Instructions

1. Make the puff pastry dough but do not add salt. (Feta cheese is quite salty already.)
2. Crumble the Feta cheese and combine it in mixing bowl together with the paprika, milk and chopped mint/parsley.
3. Beat one egg until it is in a foamy texture and add it to the Feta bowl; mix well, mashing it all up with a fork.
4. Dust a silicone pastry mat and rolling pin with a little sesame flour, place chilled pastry dough over the mat and stretch it out to cover a large baking sheet.
5. Cut into 9 sections (2 equal cuts along the longest side and 2 equal cuts along the shortest side).
6. Preheat the oven to 220° C.
7. Put a spoonful of filling on each pastry section alongside the long edge.
8. Beat the other unused egg and brush a little along the opposite edge, then roll the pastry as tightly as possible.
9. Place the rolls onto an oven rack lined with non-stick baking paper or a silicone baking mat, seams face down.
10. Brush each roll with the beaten egg.
11. Then bake for about 17-20 minutes, until golden-brown and caramelized.
12. Let the rolls cool and firm up before serving reheating them if you prefer them warm.

Macros Calories: 175 Fat: 14g Net Carbs: 0.9g Protein: 10g

86. Keto Pastry with Strawberry filling

Preparation time: 90 minutes
Cook time: 30 minutes
Servings:4

Ingredients:

- Strawberry Filling:
- 2 cups strawberries, sliced
- 3 tbsp. Swerve or equivalent granulated sweetener
- 1 tbsp vanilla extract

Crust:

- 1 cup superfine almond flour
- 5 tbsp. coconut flour
- 1/2 tsp xanthan gum, optional
- 1/2 tsp salt
- 1/2 cup cold butter
- 2 oz cold cream cheese
- 2 large beaten eggs, divided
- 2 tsp. vinegar
- 2 tbsp. Swerve or equivalent granulated sweetener
- 2 tbsp. Confectioners Swerve or equivalent powdered sweetener

Preparation Instructions

1. Add strawberries to a small bowl and sprinkle 3 tbsp. of sweetener on top. Add vanilla. Mix to coat. Cover bowl with plastic wrap and keep in the refrigerator until ready to use. Give the strawberries a stir every 10 minutes.
2. Add almond flour, coconut flour, xanthan gum and salt to a food processor or high powered blender. Pulse several times to mix.
3. Add butter and cream cheese and pulse several times.
4. Add 1 egg and vinegar and pulse several times until the dough is broken into crumbs. Do not process so much that the dough is smooth and combined like cookie dough.
5. Remove from the food processor or blender and form the dough into a ball.
6. Wrap the ball of dough in plastic wrap and refrigerate for 1 hour.
7. Place the dough on a large sheet of parchment paper. Put another sheet of parchment paper on top and roll out the dough. It should make an approximately 12 x 10 inch oval.
8. Strain liquid from strawberries.
9. Arrange the strawberries in one layer in the middle of the rolled out dough. You should have an outer edge of 1 1/2 – 2 inches of dough.
10. Use the bottom piece of parchment paper to gently fold the dough over the strawberries.
11. Brush the remaining lightly beaten egg onto the crust.
12. Sprinkle granulated sweetener on top of fruit and crust.
13. Carefully move the pastry and bottom sheet of parchment paper to a cookie sheet. Place the cookie sheet in the freezer to freeze for 10 minutes.
14. Pre-heat the oven to 400 F.
15. Bake for 25-30 minutes until crust is browned. At minute 15, take the pastry out of the oven and brush again with egg wash. Start checking in on the pastry at 20 minutes, because it can go from brown to burnt very quickly.
16. Allow to cool for about 10 minutes on the cookie sheet. Use a sieve to dust the pastry with powdered sweetener.

87. Keto Cream Puffs

Preparation time: 25 minutes
Cook time: 27 minutes
Servings: 1 - 2

Ingredients

- 1 large Raw egg
- ⅛ tsp Cream of Tartar
- 1-½ oz. Cream Cheese
- 1 package of Stevia Leaf Noncaloric Sweetener (green Packet)
- ½ cup Heavy Cream
- ¼ tsp Vanilla Extract
- 2 package of Stevia Leaf Noncaloric Sweetener (green Packet)

Preparation Instructions

1. Preheat an oven to 375 F and line a baking sheet with parchment paper.
2. Separate the egg. Whip the egg white and cream of tartar together until it holds stiff peaks. Then transfer the whipped egg white into a new bowl.
3. Wipe mixing bowl clean and combine the egg yolk with the cream cheese and first amount of stevia.
4. Fold egg whites into the egg yolk batter. Then, transfer the batter to a piping bag or a plastic Ziploc bag with the corner cut off. Pipe approximately 10 puffs on the sheet tray, each 2 inches wide.
5. Bake the puffs for 10 minutes. Then, without opening the oven, turn the heat down to 300 F and bake 15 more minutes. When they're done, the puffs will be golden brown and should easily shake loose on the parchment paper.
6. While the puffs are baking, make the cream. In a stand mixer, whip the heavy cream, vanilla, and stevia together until you have a stiff whipped cream. Do not overmix, or the cream will turn into butter.
7. Allow the cooked puffs to cool fully before continuing. Once cooled, slice each puff in half. Use a piping bag or plastic Ziploc bag to pipe the whipped cream into each puff.
8. Sandwich the puffs together.

Macros 68g Net Carbs 68g Total Carbs 0g Fiber
449g Fat 88g Protein

CHOCOLATES

88. Homemade Low-carb Chocolate

Preparation time: 5 minutes
Cook time: 5 minutes
Freezing time: 5 minutes
Servings: 10

Ingredients

- 100g cacao butter
- 6 tbsp cocoa powder unsweetened (48g)
- 4 tbsp powdered erythritol (32g)

Preparation Instructions

1. Melt the cacao butter in a pan, stirring continuously.
2. Mix the cocoa powder and powdered erythritol and stir until combined.
3. Add any optional extra (1 tsp orange zest/pinch cinnamon/pinch of sea salt/pinch of chili/1/3 cup (50g) low-carb granola/handful of nuts and seeds and stir
4. Fill into a silicone chocolate mold to make chocolate bars. Or pour onto parchment paper to make chocolate bark.
5. Freeze for 5 minutes or more and serve.

Macros Calories: 81kcal Carbohydrates: 1.5g Protein: 0.5g Fat: 8.7g Saturated Fat: 5.5g Fiber: 0.9g

89. Keto Chocolate Cake

Preparation time: 15 minutes
Cook Time: 15 minutes
Servings:6-8

Ingredients

- 1 1/2 cups fine almond flour
- 1/4 cup cocoa powder
- 1 tbsp Dutch cocoa
- 1/4 tsp of baking powder
- 1/2 tsp salt
- 1/3 cup water or milk of choice
- eggs, including the vegan option listed earlier in the post
- 1/3 cup granulated erythritol or regular sugar
- 1 1/2 tsp pure vanilla extract

Preparation Instructions

1. Mix all the ingredients together. Note: for a double layer cake, simply double the recipe and bake in two 8-inch pans.
2. Preheat the oven to 350 F. Grease an 8-inch pan or line with parchment.
3. Stir all ingredients well, then spread into the pan.
4. Bake 14 minutes on the center rack. Let it cool completely before frosting.

Macros Calories: 130 Total Fat: 9g Saturated Fat: 0.9g Sodium: 175mg

90. Low-carb Chocolate cookies with Sesame Seeds

Preparation time: 10 minutes
Cook time: 15 minutes
Servings: 6-8

Ingredients

Cream Together

- 1/4 cup (2 oz/57 g) butter, softened
- 2 tbsp. (2 oz/57 g) cream cheese, softened
- 1/3 cup Sukrin 1 (or Swerve Granulated)
- 1 large egg, cold
- 1 tsp vanilla
- 1/2 tsp stevia glycerite

Stir Together

- 3/4 cup almond flour (75 g)
- 1/3 cup (30 g) Sukrin Sesame Flour (or 1/4 cup coconut flour)
- 2 tbsp. (30 ml) unsweetened cocoa powder
- 1/2 tsp espresso powder or instant coffee granules
- 1/4 tsp salt
- 1/4 tsp xanthan gum

Optional Chocolate Drizzle

- 2 oz. (57 g) dark chocolate such as Lily's Chocolate Chips
- 1/4 cup (59 ml) heavy cream
- 1 tbsp (15 ml) butter
- 1 tsp. (10 ml) sesame seeds

Preparation Instructions

1. In a medium bowl, mix the butter and cream cheese. Add the sweetener and salt, creaming until it is light and fluffy. Mix the egg, vanilla and stevia glycerite, and beat them until they are incorporated.
2. In a small bowl, blend all of the dry ingredients together with a large wire whisk.
3. Add all the dry ingredients to the medium bowl and mix completely.
4. Scrape the dough onto a piece of plastic wrap or wax paper, and form into a log. Fold the wax paper over the dough and shape in
5. Refrigerate for 6 hours.
6. Preheat oven to 350 F and place the rack into the middle position. Line a baking sheet with parchment. Slice the cookie dough into 16 even cookies and place onto the parchment. They won't spread, so if you want to flatten them out, use a small piece of wax paper and a flat bottomed glass to do so. Bake 15-20 minutes.
7. Place the heavy cream, butter and chocolate (chopped or chips) into a microwaveable bowl and heat at 30 second intervals until melted. Blend completely with a small whisk. Scrape the chocolate into a small Ziploc bag and snip off a tiny piece of the corner. Squeeze the chocolate over the cookies in a pleasing pattern. Sprinkle with sesame seeds.

Macros Calories: 102kcal Carbohydrates: 3g Protein: 3g Fat: 9g Fiber: 1g

91. Low-carb Chocolate Truffles

Preparation time:10 minutes
Cook time: 6 minutes
Servings: 20

Ingredients

- 1 cup (170 g) Lily's Sugar Free Chocolate Chips
- 3/4 cup (177 ml) heavy cream
- 1 tbsp butter
- 1 tbsp low-carb powdered sugar
- 1 tsp brandy
- 1/4 tsp vanilla extract

Preparation Instructions

1. Pour the heavy cream into a microwave-safe glass bowl big enough to accommodate the chocolate chips and cream with room for stirring.
2. Add 4 tbsp. of sweetener and stir to dissolve. Add the butter and sugar-free chocolate chips and microwave at full power for 1 minute.
3. Let it sit for 5 minutes and stir gently with a whisk until fully incorporated. Add the vanilla and brandy and stir.
4. Let it cool, then cover and refrigerate for a few hours until firm or overnight.
5. Scoop the firm chocolate ganache from the bowl with a small dinner spoon or a melon baller and place onto the wax paper.
6. Continue until the ganache is gone. If the ganache is too firm, let it warm up for 30 minutes to 1 hour before scooping.
7. Roll each portion of ganache into round "truffles".
8. The truffles can be rolled in chopped nuts, grated chocolate, sesame seeds, coconut, sprinkles, crushed freeze-dried fruit, matcha powder, or unsweetened cocoa powder.

Macros Calories: 58kcal Carbohydrates: 7g Protein: 1g | Fat: 5g Saturated Fat: 3g. Monounsaturated Fat: 1g Cholesterol: 10mg Sodium: 3mg Potassium: 5mg
Fiber: 5g Vitamin A: 100IU

KETO COOKIES

92. Chocolate and Butter Cookies

Preparation time: 10 minutes
Cook time: 20 minutes
Servings: 15

Ingredients
- 2/3 cup nut butter of choice
- 2/3 cup erythritol
- 1 egg
- 1/3 cup butter, melted
- 5 tbsp. coconut flour
- 1/3 cup sugar-free dark chocolate chips or chunks

Preparation Instructions:
1. Preheat the oven to 350 F. Grease a baking sheet.
2. In a bowl, combine first 5 ingredients. Mix well. Add the chocolate chips and make the dough.
3. Place the dough in the bowl in the freezer for 10 minutes.
4. Remove from the freezer. With a spoon, scoop 1 tbsp. dough onto the cookie sheet.
5. Bake until browned, about 15 to 20 minutes.
6. Remove from oven and cool completely.

Macros:
Calories: 120
Fat: 11 g
Carb: 5 g
Protein: 3 g

93. Chocolate Biscotti

Preparation time: 10 minutes
Cook time: 12 minutes
Servings: 8

Ingredients
- 2 tbsp. chia seeds
- 2 cup almonds
- 1 egg
- ¼ cup of coconut oil
- ¼ cup coconut, shredded
- 2 tbsp. stevia
- ¼ cup of cocoa powder
- A pinch of salt
- 1 tsp. baking soda

Preparation Instructions:
1. In a food processor, mix chia seeds with almonds and blend well.
2. Add egg, coconut, coconut oil, cocoa powder, salt, baking soda, and stevia and blend well.
3. Shape 8 biscotti pieces out of this dough.
4. Place on a lined baking sheet.
5. Bake in the oven at 350 F for 12 minutes.

Macros:
Calories: 200
Fat: 2g
Carb: 3g
Protein: 4g

94. Chocolate Cookies

Preparation time: 10 minutes
Cook time: 40 minutes
Servings: 12

Ingredients

- 1 tsp. vanilla extract
- ½ cup ghee
- 1 egg
- 2 tbsp. erythritol, powdered
- ¼ cup Swerve
- A pinch of salt
- 2 cups almond flour
- ½ cup chocolate chips, unsweetened

Preparation Instructions:

1. Heat a pan with ghee over medium heat. Stir until it browns.
2. Remove from heat and set aside for 5 minutes.
3. In a bowl, mix the egg with vanilla extract, erythritol, and Swerve and stir.
4. Add melted ghee, salt, flour, and half of the chocolate chips, and stir everything.
5. Transfer this to a pan; spread the remaining chocolate chips on top.
6. Bake in the oven at 350 F for 30 minutes.
7. Slice when cold and serve.

Macros:
Calories: 230
Fat: 12g
Carb: 4g
Protein: 5g

95. Almond Butter Cookies

Preparation time: 5 minutes
Cook time: 10 minutes
Servings: 10

Ingredients:

- 1 cup almond flour
- 1 tsp vanilla
- ¼ cup erythritol
- ¼ cup butter softened
- Pinch of salt

Preparation Instructions:

1. Preheat the oven to 350 F/ 180 C.
2. Line a baking tray with parchment paper and set aside.
3. Add all ingredients into a food processor and process until dough is formed, 2 minutes.
4. Make cookies from dough and place on the prepared baking tray.
5. Bake in preheated oven for 10 minutes.
6. Remove cookies from oven and allow to cool completely.

Macros: Calories: 106; Total Fat: 10.2g; Saturated Fat: 3.3g; Protein: 2.5g; Carbs: 2.5g; Fiber: 1.2g; Sugar: 0.5g

96. Crunchy Shortbread Cookies

Preparation time: 10 minutes
Cook time: 10 minutes
Servings: 6

Ingredients:

- 1 ¼ cup almond flour
- ½ tsp vanilla
- 3 tbsp butter, softened
- ¼ cup Swerve
- Pinch of salt

Preparation Instructions:

1. Preheat the oven to 350 F/ 180 C.
2. In a bowl, mix together almond flour, swerve, and salt.
3. Add vanilla and butter and mix until dough is formed.
4. Make cookies from mixture and place on a baking tray.
5. Bake in preheated oven for 10 minutes.
6. Allow to cool completely then serve.

Macros: Calories: 185; Total Fat: 17.4g; Saturated Fat: 4.5g; Protein: 5.1g; Carbs: 5.1g; Fiber: 2.5g

97. Cream Cheese Cookies

Preparation time: 10 minutes
Cook time: 15 minutes
Servings: 24

Ingredients:

- 1 egg white
- 3 cups almond flour
- 1 ½ tsp vanilla
- ½ cup erythritol
- 2 oz cream cheese, softened
- ¼ cup butter softened
- Pinch of salt

Preparation Instructions:

1. Preheat the oven to 350 F/ 180 C.
2. Line cookie sheet with parchment paper and set aside.
3. Add butter, sweetener, and cream cheese in a food processor and process until fluffy.
4. Add egg white, vanilla, and salt and process well to combine.
5. Add almond flour and process well to combine.
6. Make cookies from mixture and place on prepared cookie sheet.
7. Bake for 15 minutes.
8. Allow to cool completely then serve.

Macros: Calories: 107 Total Fat: 9.7g; Saturated Fat: 2.2g; Protein: 3.4g; Carbs: 3.1g; Fiber: 1.5g;

98. Gingersnap Cookies

Preparation time: 10 minutes
Cook time: 10 minutes
Servings: 8

Ingredients:

- 1 egg
- ½ tsp vanilla
- 1/8 tsp ground cloves
- ¼ tsp ground nutmeg
- ¼ tsp ground cinnamon
- ½ tsp ground ginger
- 1 tsp of baking powder
- ¾ cup erythritol
- 2/4 cup butter, melted
- 1 ½ cups almond flour
- Pinch of salt

Preparation Instructions:

1. In a mixing bowl, mix together all dry ingredients.
2. In another bowl, mix together all wet ingredients.
3. Add dry ingredients to the wet ingredients and mix until dough-like mixture is formed.
4. Cover and place in the refrigerator for 30 minutes.
5. Preheat the oven to 350 F/ 180 C.
6. Line a baking tray with parchment paper and set aside.
7. Make cookies from dough and place on the prepared baking tray.
8. Bake for 10-15 minutes.
9. Serve and enjoy.

Macros: Calories: 232; Total Fat: 22.6g; Saturated Fat: 8.2g; Protein: 5.3g; Carbs: 5.1g; Fiber: 2.3g

99. Easy Coconut Cookies

Preparation time: 10 minutes
Cook time: 10 minutes
Servings: 40

Ingredients:

- 4 cups unsweetened shredded coconut
- 1/2 cup unsweetened coconut milk
- 1/4 cup erythritol
- 1/4 tsp vanilla

Preparation Instructions:

1. Add all ingredients to a food processor and process until sticky.
2. Transfer mixture to the large bowl.
3. Make a small ball from mixture and place on a plate.
4. Press each ball lightly into a cookie shape and place in the fridge until firm.

Macros: Calories: 79; Total Fat: 7.1g; Saturated Fat: 6.2g; Protein: 0.9g; Carbs: 2.6g; Fiber: 1.7g

100. Simple Chocolate Cookies

Preparation time: 5 minutes
Cook time: 10 minutes
Servings: 20

Ingredients:
- 3 tbsp ground chia
- 1 cup almond flour
- 2 tbsp chocolate protein powder
- 1 cup sunflower seed butter

Preparation Instructions:
1. Preheat the oven to 350 F/ 180 C.
2. Spray baking sheet with cooking spray and set aside.
3. In a large bowl, add all ingredients and mix until combined.
4. Make small balls from mixture and place on a prepared baking sheet.
5. Press lightly into a cookie shape.
6. Bake for 10 minutes.
7. Allow to cool completely then serve.

Macros: Calories: 111; Total Fat: 9.3g; Saturated Fat: 0.9g, Protein: 4g; Carbs: 5.2g; Fiber: 1g

101. Vanilla Green Tea Cookies

Preparation time: 10 minutes
Cook time: 25 minutes
Servings: 10

Ingredients:
- ½ cup coconut flour
- 1 tsp green tea powder
- 1 cup coconut milk
- 2 eggs, whisked
- ½ cup ghee, melted
- 2 tbsp. stevia
- 2 tsp. vanilla extract
- 2 tsp. baking powder

Preparation Instructions:
1. In a bowl, mix the coconut flour with the green tea powder, milk and other ingredients, and whisk well.
2. Shape 10 balls from this mix, place them on a lined baking sheet, flatten them, introduce in the oven at 350 F and bake for 25 minutes.
3. Serve cold.

Macros: Calories 130, fat 2, fiber 2, carbs 4, protein 3

102. Orange and Chocolate Cookies

Preparation time: 10 minutes
Cook time: 20 minutes
Servings: 10

Ingredients:
- 4 eggs, whisked
- ½ cup orange juice
- 1 and ½ cups almond flour
- ½ cup chocolate, unsweetened and melted
- 1 tbsp stevia
- 1 tsp vanilla extract
- 1 tsp of baking powder
- 2 tbsp. orange zest, grated

Preparation Instructions:
1. In a blender, combine the eggs with the orange juice, almond flour and other ingredients and pulse well.
2. Pour this onto a baking sheet lined with parchment paper, spread and bake at 360 F for 20 minutes.
3. Cut with a cookie cutter and serve cold.

Macros: Calories 200, fat 13, fiber 2, carbs 5, protein 8

103. Berry and Avocado Cookies

Preparation time: 10 minutes
Cook time: 25 minutes
Servings: 8
Ingredients:
- 2 oz. coconut oil, melted
- 1 and ½ cups coconut flour
- 1 avocado, peeled, pitted and mashed
- 1 cup blackberries, pureed
- 2 tbsp. stevia
- ½ tsp of baking powder
- 1 tsp vanilla extract
- 3 eggs, whisked

Preparation Instructions:
1. In a food processor, combine the melted coconut oil with the avocado, flour and other ingredients and pulse well.
2. Spread on a baking sheet lined with parchment paper, cut with a cookie cutter and bake at 360 F for 25 minutes.
3. Serve cold.
Macros: Calories 100, fat 10, fiber 1, carbs 3, protein 2

104. Almond, Cocoa and Vanilla Cookies

Preparation time: 10 minutes
Cook time: 25 minutes
Servings: 10
Ingredients:
- ½ cup ghee, melted
- ¼ cup almonds, chopped
- 1 tbsp cocoa powder
- 1 cup almond flour
- 1 cup almond milk
- ½ tsp vanilla extract
- 1 tsp of baking powder
- 2 tbsp. stevia
- 3 eggs, whisked

Preparation Instructions:
1. In a bowl, combine the ghee with the almonds, cocoa powder and the other ingredients and whisk well.
2. Take spoonfuls of this mix, arrange on a baking sheet lined with parchment paper, flatten a bit and bake at 360 F for 25 minutes.
3. Serve cold.
Macros: Calories 450, fat 34, fiber 7, carbs 10, protein 20

105. Psyllium Cookies

Preparation time: 10 minutes
Cook time: 30 minutes
Servings: 8
Ingredients:
- ½ cup almond flour
- ½ cup almond milk
- 1/3 cup psyllium husks
- 2 tbsp. stevia
- 1 tsp of baking powder
- 4 eggs
- 1 tsp cinnamon powder

Preparation Instructions:
1. In a bowl, combine the almond flour with the milk and the other ingredients and whisk well.
2. Shape 8 cookies, arrange them on a lined baking sheet, flatten them and cook at 350 For 30 minutes.
3. Serve cold.
Macros: Calories 100, fat 3, fiber 3, carbs 6, protein 6

106. Coconut Chips Cookies

Preparation time: 10 minutes
Cook time: 30 minutes
Servings: 10
Ingredients:
- 3 tbsp. stevia
- 1 cup heavy cream
- 1 cup coconut flour
- 3 eggs, whisked
- 1 tsp of baking powder
- ½ cup coconut chips, unsweetened
- 1 tsp vanilla extract

Preparation Instructions:
1. In a bowl, combine ingredients and whisk well.
2. Take spoonfuls of this mix, arrange on a baking sheet lined with parchment paper, flatten them and cook at 360 F for 30 minutes.
3. Serve cold.

Macros: Calories 245, fat 34, fiber 2, carbs 6, protein 2

107. Mixed Fruit Cookies

Preparation time: 10 minutes
Cook time: 30 minutes
Servings: 12
Ingredients:
- 2 tbsp. stevia
- 4 eggs, whisked
- 1 cup almond flour
- 1 cup almond milk
- ½ cup heavy cream
- 1 tsp of baking powder
- ½ cup blueberries
- ½ cup blackberries
- 1 avocado, peeled, pitted and cubed
- 1 plum, pitted and chopped
- 1 tsp vanilla extract

Preparation Instructions:
1. In a bowl, mix ingredients and whisk well.
2. Take spoonfuls of this mix, arrange on a baking sheet lined with parchment paper, flatten them and bake at 350 F for 30 minutes.
3. Serve cold.

Macros: Calories 55, fat 6, fiber 1, carbs 2, protein 1

108. Pecan Cookies

Preparation time: 10 minutes
Cook time: 30 minutes
Servings: 8
Ingredients:
- 1 cup pecans, chopped
- 1 cup almond flour
- 1 and ½ cups almond milk
- ¼ cup ghee, melted
- 2 tbsp. stevia
- 1 tsp nutmeg, ground
- 1 tsp of baking powder
- 1 tsp vanilla extract
- 3 eggs, whisked

Preparation Instructions:
1. In a bowl, combine ingredients and whisk well.
2. Spread on a lined baking sheet, place in the oven at 300 F and bake for 30 minutes.
3. Cut with a cookie cutter, cool down and serve.

Macros: Calories 120, fat 2, fiber 2, carbs 4, protein 7

109. Macadamia and Coconut Cookies

Preparation time: 10 minutes
Cook time: 30 minutes
Servings: 4
Ingredients:
- ½ cup macadamia nuts, chopped
- 1 cup coconut flour
- 1 and ½ cups coconut milk
- 2 eggs, whisked
- 1 tsp of baking soda
- 1 tsp vanilla extract
- ¼ cup ghee, melted
- 1 tsp vanilla stevia

Preparation Instructions:
1. In a bowl, combine the ingredients and whisk well.
2. Take spoonfuls of this mix, arrange on a baking sheet lined with parchment paper, flatten them and bake at 360 F for 30 minutes.
3. Serve cold.

Macros: Calories 120, fat 1, fiber 2, carbs 4, protein 2

110. Dark Chocolate and Vanilla Cookies

Preparation time: 10 minutes
Cook time: 30 minutes
Servings: 12

Ingredients:
- 4 oz. ghee, melted
- 1 cup coconut flour
- 1 cup coconut milk
- 4 oz. dark chocolate, sugar free and melted
- 1 tsp of baking soda
- 1 tsp vanilla extract
- 1 tbsp stevia
- 2 eggs, whisked

Preparation Instructions:
1. In a bowl, mix the ingredients and whisk well.
2. Take spoonfuls of this mix, arrange on a baking sheet lined with parchment paper, flatten them and cook at 365 F for 30 minutes.
3. Serve warm.

Macros: Calories 176, fat 15, fiber 2, carbs 5, protein 3

111. Allspice Nut Cookies

Preparation time: 10 minutes
Cook time: 30 minutes
Servings: 8

Ingredients:
- 2 tbsp. almonds, chopped
- 2 tbsp. walnuts, chopped
- 1 cup coconut milk
- 1 cup coconut flour
- 1 tbsp stevia
- 1 tsp allspice, ground
- 1 tsp of baking powder
- 2 eggs, whisked

Preparation Instructions:
1. In a bowl, mix the almonds with the walnuts, milk and other ingredients and whisk well.
2. Spread this onto a baking sheet, lined with parchment paper, and bake at 360 F for 30 minutes.
3. Cut with a cookie cutter and serve cold.

Macros: Calories 140, fat 2, fiber 1, carbs 2, protein 4

112. Peanut Butter Cookies

Preparation time: 10 minutes
Cook time: 25 minutes
Servings: 2

Ingredients:
- 2 tbsp. ghee, melted
- 1 tbsp stevia
- 1 cup peanut butter, melted
- 1 cup almond flour
- ½ cup almond milk
- 2 eggs, whisked
- ¼ tsp vanilla extract
- 1 tsp of baking powder

Preparation Instructions:
1. In a bowl, combine the ingredients and whisk well.
2. Take spoonfuls and arrange on a baking sheet lined with parchment paper, flatten and bake at 370 F for 25 minutes.
3. Cool down and serve.

Macros: Calories 344, fat 35.1, fiber 3.4, carbs 8.3, protein 4.5

113. Ginger and Vanilla Cookies

Preparation time: 5 minutes
Cook time: 25 minutes
Servings: 10

Ingredients:
- 2 tbsp. swerve
- 1 cup almond milk
- 1 cup almond flour
- 3 eggs, whisked
- 1 tbsp ginger, grated
- 1 tsp vanilla extract
- 1 tsp of baking powder

Preparation Instructions:
1. In a bowl, mix the almond milk with the flour and the other ingredients and whisk well.
2. Take spoonfuls of this mix, arrange on a baking sheet lined with parchment paper, flatten them and bake at 360 F for 25 minutes.
3. Cool the ginger cookies down and serve.

Macros: Calories 400, fat 23, fiber 4, carbs 6, protein 7

114. Classic Cookies

Preparation time: 10 minutes
Cook time: 20 minutes
Servings: 15

Ingredients:
- 3 eggs
- 2 cups almond flour
- 1/3 tsp vanilla extract
- A pinch of cinnamon
- 2 tsp erythritol

Preparation Instructions:
1. Preheat oven to 350 F.
2. Place parchment paper over a baking sheet.
3. In a small bowl, add the vanilla extract and the eggs and whisk together thoroughly.
4. In another bowl, combine the cinnamon, almond flour, and erythritol. Pour it into the egg mixture and stir to combine.
5. Use a spoon to scoop the cookies out onto a baking tray.
6. Put the cookies in the oven and bake for 20 minutes.
7. Remove the cookies from the oven and cool completely before serving.

Macros:
Calories: 51
Fat: 0.9g
Carbohydrates: 8.6g
Protein: 2.5g

115. Cottage Cheese Cookies

Preparation time: 10 minutes
Cook time: 30 minutes
Servings: 15

Ingredients:
- 8 oz cottage cheese
- 2 cups almond flour
- 1 cup water
- 1 tbsp lemon juice
- 1 tsp stevia

Preparation Instructions:
1. Preheat oven to 350 F.
2. Place parchment paper over a baking sheet.
3. In a large bowl, combine the stevia, almond flour, water, and cottage cheese.
4. Add the lemon juice and stir to combine.
5. Scoop the cookies out onto the baking tray.
6. Bake for 30 minutes.

Macros:
Calories: 120
Fat: 1.2g
Carbohydrates: 6g
Protein: 5.2g

116. Crispy Cookies

Preparation time: 10 minutes
Cook time: 20 minutes
Servings: 15

Ingredients:

- 2 eggs
- 1 tbsp soy flour
- 3 tbsp almond flour
- 1-2 tsp coconut chips
- 1/2 cup milk
- 1 tsp of baking soda
- 1 tsp vanilla extract
- Any sweetener of choice

Preparation Instructions:

1. Preheat the oven to 350 F.
2. Place parchment paper over a baking sheet and lay 12 silicone molds on it.
3. Combine all the ingredients together in a large bowl and leave for 15 minutes.
4. Pour the dough into the silicone molds and bake for 20 minutes.

Macros:

Calories: 104
Fat: 9g
Carbohydrates: 11g
Protein: 12.3g

117. Cream Stuffed Cookies

Preparation time: 10 minutes
Cook time: 30 minutes
Servings: 15

Ingredients:

For the cookies:

- 1 1/2 cups almond flour
- 1/3 cup cocoa powder
- 1/8 cup black cocoa powder
- 3/4 tsp kosher salt
- 1/2 tsp xanthan gum
- 1/2 tsp of baking powder
- 1/4 tsp espresso powder
- 1/3 cup soft unsalted butter
- 1/2 cup erythritol
- 1 egg

For the cream:

- 1/4 cup soft butter
- 1 tbsp coconut oil
- 1 1/2 tsp vanilla extract
- A pinch of kosher salt
- 1/2 cup sweetener of choice

Preparation Instructions:

1. Preheat the oven to 350 F.
2. Place parchment paper over a baking sheet.
3. In a medium sized bowl combine the espresso powder, baking soda, salt, xanthan gum, cocoa powder, and almond flour, whisk to combine and set to the side.
4. In another large bowl, combine the butter and the sweetener and use an electric handheld mixer to whisk together until the sweetener has completely dissolved.
5. Add the egg to the butter mixture and use a spoon to mix slightly.
6. Add half the flour mixture and use the electric handheld mixer to whisk together, add the rest and continue to whisk until a dough is formed.
7. Use saran wrap to wrap the cookie dough and put it in the fridge for an hour.
8. Remove the dough from the fridge, remove the saran wrap and roll it out on a floured chopping board.
9. Use a cookie cutter to cut out the cookies and then transfer them onto the baking tray.
10. Put the baking tray in the freezer for 15 minutes.
11. Remove the baking tray from the freezer and bake for 12 minutes.
12. Once cooked, take the cookies out of the oven and allow them to cool down completely.
13. Make the filling by taking a medium sized bowl, add the coconut oil, and butter and whisk with the electric mixer.
14. Add a pinch of salt and vanilla extract and continue to whisk.
15. Add the sweetener and continue to whisk until mixture becomes fluffy and light in texture.
16. Spread the cream onto half of the cookies, and top them with the other half.
17. Put the cookies in the fridge until they set and then serve.

Macros:

Calories: 86
Fat: 8g
Carbohydrates: 2g
Protein: 1g

118. Minty Cookies

Preparation time: 10 minutes
Cook time: 20 minutes
Servings: 15

Ingredients:

- 2 1/4 cups almond flour
- 3 tbsp coconut flour
- 4 tbsp cacao powder
- 1 tsp of baking powder
- 1 1/2 tsp xanthan powder
- 1/4 tsp salt
- 1/2 cup unsalted softened butter
- 1 egg
- 1 tsp vanilla extract
- 4 oz cream cheese
- 1 cup sweetener of choice
- 1 tsp peppermint extract

Preparation Instructions:

1. Preheat the oven to 350 F.
2. Place parchment paper over a baking sheet.
3. In a large bowl, combine the xanthan gum, cacao powder, baking powder, coconut flour, almond flour, and salt.
4. In another bowl, combine 6 tbsp. of butter and the sweetener and whisk together with an electric hand-held mixer until it becomes fluffy.
5. Add the vanilla extract and the egg and whisk again.
6. Combine the dry and the wet ingredients and continue to whisk until mixture turns into a dough.
7. Roll the dough out on a floured cutting board until it is around 1/8 of an inch in thickness.
8. Use a cookie cutter, arrange the cookies on the baking tray and bake for 12 minutes.
9. Combine the remaining butter, and cream cheese in a bowl and whisk together thoroughly.
10. Add the peppermint extract and continue to whisk together.
11. Once the cookies have cooled down, spread the cream on top of half of the cookies and then put the other half on top of the cream.

Macros:

Calories: 120
Fat: 11.3g
Carbohydrates: 1.8g
Protein: 3.1g

119. Mighty Minty Cookies

Preparation time: 40 minutes
Cook time: 12 minutes
Servings: 15

Ingredients:
- 6 tbsp melted butter
- 2 cups almond flour, superfine
- 1/2 cup erythritol
- 1/2 cup chopped pistachios
- 1 tsp vanilla extract

Preparation Instructions:
1. Preheat the oven to 350 F.
2. Place parchment paper over a baking sheet.
3. In a medium sized bowl, combine all the ingredients and use a hand-held electric mixer to whisk together thoroughly.
4. Use saran wrap to wrap the dough and put it in the fridge for 30 minutes.
5. Take the dough out of the fridge and remove the saran wrap.
6. Roll out the dough on a floured cutting board.
7. Cut the cookies out using a cookie cutter and arrange them on the baking tray.
8. Put the cookies in the oven and bake for 12 minutes.

Macros:
Calories: 135
Fat: 12g
Carbohydrates: 2g
Protein: 4g

120. Dipped Chocolate Cookies

Preparation time: 40 minutes
Cook time: 30 minutes
Servings: 15

Ingredients:
- 1 1/2 cups almond flour
- 1/4 cup almond butter
- 2 tbsp swerve
- 1 large egg
- 1 tsp vanilla powder
- 1 tbsp virgin coconut oil
- 1 tbsp coconut butter
- 1 tsp of baking powder
- A pinch of salt
- 90g dark chocolate

Preparation Instructions:
1. Preheat the oven to 350 F.
2. Place parchment paper over a baking sheet.
3. In a large bowl, combine the baking powder, vanilla, swerve, almond flour, and salt.
4. Add the egg, coconut butter, and coconut oil and whisk together using an electric mixer to form a dough.
5. Put the mixture in a sandwich bag and refrigerate for 30 minutes.
6. Remove the dough from the fridge, take it out of the sandwich bag and roll the dough out on a floured chopping board.
7. Use a cookie cutter to cut out the cookies and arrange them onto the baking tray.
8. Put the baking tray in the oven and bake for 30 minutes.
9. Melt the chocolate in the microwave.
10. Dip half of each cookie into the chocolate, place them onto a wire rack and put them in the fridge until they set and then serve.

Macros:
Calories: 211
Fat: 18.8g
Carbohydrates: 3.3g
Protein: 6g

121. Snickerdoodle Cookies

Preparation time: 10 minutes
Cook time: 15 minutes
Servings: 15

Ingredients:

For the cookies:

- 2 cups almond flour, superfine
- 1/2 cup softened salted butter
- A pinch of kosher salt
- 3/4 cup granulated erythritol
- 1/2 tsp of baking soda

For the coating:

- 2 tbsp granulated erythritol
- 1 tsp ground cinnamon

Preparation Instructions:

1. Preheat the oven to 350 F.
2. Place parchment paper over a baking sheet.
3. In a medium sized bowl combine all the cookie ingredients and whisk with an electric mixer until a dough is formed.
4. Roll the dough into balls.
5. On a small plate, combine the cinnamon and sweetener.
6. Roll the balls into the mix and arrange them onto the baking tray.
7. Put the cookies in the oven and bake for 15 minutes.

Macros:

Calories: 131
Fat: 13g
Carbohydrates: 1.5g
Protein: 3g

122. Sugar Lemon Cookies

Preparation time: 10 minutes
Cook time: 10 minutes
Servings: 15
Ingredients:
For the cookies:
- 3/4 cup almond flour, fine
- 1 tbsp coconut flour
- 1/2 tsp xanthan gum
- 1/2 tsp of baking powder
- 1/4 tsp salt
- 1/3 cup swerve
- 1/4 cup soft butter
- 1 large egg
- 1 egg yolk
- 1 tbsp fresh lemon juice
- 1 tbsp lemon zest, freshly grated
- 1 tsp vanilla extract

For the icing:
- 8 tbsp powdered swerve
- 2 tbsp fresh lemon juice

Preparation Instructions:
1. Preheat the oven to 350 F.
2. Place parchment paper over a baking sheet.
3. Make the cookies by combining the xanthan gum, almond flour, baking powder, coconut flour, and salt in a medium sized bowl.
4. In a separate bowl, combine the butter and swerve and use a handheld electric mixer to whisk together until it becomes creamy.
5. Add the egg yolk, egg, lemon zest, lemon juice, and vanilla extract and whisk together thoroughly.
6. Add the flour mixture in half a cup at a time, and use a handheld electric mixer to combine.
7. Use hands to make balls and arrange them onto the baking tray. Flatten the cookies out using the palm of hands.
8. Bake the cookies for 10 minutes.
9. Once cooked, remove the cookies from the oven and allow them to cool down completely.
10. While the cookies are cooling down, you can start making the icing. In a small bowl, combine the lemon juice and the swerve and whisk together to combine.
11. Use a spatula to spread the icing over the cookies and serve.

Macros:
Calories: 196
Fat: 16.6g
Carbohydrates: 10g
Protein: 5g

123. Orange Cookies

Preparation time: 10 minutes
Cook time: 10 minutes
Servings: 15

Ingredients:

- 1/2 cup coconut flour
- 1 1/2 tsp of baking powder
- 1/4 tsp of baking soda
- 3 large eggs
- 1/3 cup soft butter
- 3/4 cup swerve
- 1/2 cup walnuts, chopped
- 1 1/2 tsp orange zest, grated

Preparation Instructions:

1. Preheat the oven to 350 F.
2. Place parchment paper over a baking sheet.
3. In a large bowl, combine the baking powder, flour, and baking soda and stir to combine.
4. In another large bowl, combine the butter, eggs, and swerve and use a handheld electric mixer to whisk the ingredients together thoroughly.
5. Add the butter mixture to the flour mixture and use the handheld mixture to combine until the mixture turns into a dough.
6. Fold in the orange zest, and walnuts.
7. Roll the dough into small balls and arrange them on the baking tray, and flatten them slightly.
8. Bake the cookies for 10 minutes.

Macros:

Calories: 52
Fat: 5.3g
Carbohydrates: 0.4g
Protein: 1g

124. Bacon Chocolate Cookies

Preparation time: 10 minutes
Cook time: 35 minutes
Servings: 15

Ingredients:

- 5 slices of bacon
- 3/4 cup Yacon syrup
- 3 cups almond flour, blanched
- 1 tsp of baking soda
- 1 tsp salt
- 1/2 cup melted coconut oil
- 2 large eggs
- 1 tsp vanilla extract
- 1 1/2 cups cacao dark chocolate

Preparation Instructions:

1. Preheat the oven to 350 F.
2. Place parchment paper over a baking sheet.
3. Combine 1/4 cup of the Yacon syrup and the bacon in a bowl and toss to coat.
4. Lay the bacon onto the baking sheet and bake for 20 minutes.
5. Line a plate with a paper towel and place the bacon on it once cooked and leave it to cool down.
6. Once the bacon has cooled down, crumble it up with hands.
7. Prepare another baking tray with parchment paper.
8. In a large bowl, combine the baking soda, flour, and salt and stir to combine.
9. In another large bowl, combine the eggs, remaining Yacon syrup, coconut oil, and vanilla extract and use a hand-held electric mixer to combine.
10. Combine the mixtures together and use the mixer to whisk.
11. Fold in the cacao dark chocolate and bacon.
12. Use a tbsp to scoop balls onto the baking tray, and flatten them out with the palm of hands.
13. Bake for 15 minutes.

Macros:

Calories: 162
Fat: 13.1g
Carbohydrates: 10g
Protein: 5g

125. Cinnabon Cookies

Preparation time: 10 minutes
Cook time: 28 minutes
Servings: 15

Ingredients:

For the cookies:
- 2 tbsp softened butter
- 1 tbsp egg white
- 1/2 tsp vanilla extract
- 2 tbsp almond flour
- 1/2 scoop unflavored protein
- 1 tbsp truvia
- 1 1/2 tbsp Splenda
- 1/8 tsp of baking soda
- 1/4 tsp xanthan gum
- 1/8 tsp salt

For the filling:
- 1/2 tsp butter
- 1/2 tsp cinnamon

For the frosted cream cheese:
- 1 tbsp coconut oil
- 2 tbsp cream cheese
- 1 tsp egg white
- 1/8 tsp vanilla extract
- 2 tbsp Splenda

Preparation Instructions:
1. Preheat the oven to 350 F.
2. Place parchment paper over a baking sheet.
3. For the cookies combine the almond flour, protein, truvia, salt, Splenda, and baking soda in a medium sized bowl.
4. Combine the butter, egg white, vanilla extract, and xanthan gum in a small bowl and whisk with a hand-held electric mixer.
5. Combine the two mixtures and use an electric mixer to whisk together until the ingredients form a dough.
6. Cover the dough in saran wrap and put it in the fridge for 20 minutes.
7. Take the dough out of the fridge, remove the saran wrap and roll it out on a floured chopping board.
8. Brush the dough with some butter and sprinkle cinnamon over the top.
9. Roll the dough to form into a rectangular block.
10. Cover the dough in the saran wrap and place it in the fridge for 20 minutes.
11. For the frosting put the coconut oil and cream cheese in a microwavable bowl and heat for 30 seconds.
12. Remove the bowl from the microwave and stir in Splenda, egg white, and vanilla.
13. Remove the dough from fridge and slice it into 7 pieces and arrange them on the baking tray.
14. Put the baking tray in the oven and cook for 8 minutes.
15. Remove the cookies from the oven and let cool completely.
16. Drizzle frosting over the top and serve.

Macros:
Calories: 75
Fat: 6g
Carbohydrates: 2.4g
Protein: 7g

126. Nutty Cookies

Preparation time: 10 minutes
Cook time: 15 minutes
Servings: 15

Ingredients:
- 1/4 cup coconut oil
- 4 tbsp soft butter
- 2 tbsp swerve
- 4 egg yolks
- 1 cup dark cacao dark chocolate
- 1 cup coconut flakes
- 3/4 cup walnuts roughly chopped

Preparation Instructions:
1. Preheat the oven to 350 F.
2. Place parchment paper over a baking sheet.
3. Combine the egg yolks, sweetener, butter, coconut oil, walnuts, coconut, and cacao dark chocolate in a large bowl and stir to combine.
4. Spoon the batter out onto the baking tray and bake for 15 minutes.

Macros:
Calories: 135
Fat: 6.3g
Carbohydrates: 7.2g
Protein: 4g

127. Espresso Cookies

Preparation time: 10 minutes
Cook time: 15 minutes
Servings: 15

Ingredients:
For the espresso cookies:
- 1/2 cup melted butter
- 1/4 cup espresso
- 1 cup almond flour
- 1/4 cup coconut flour
- 1/4 cup erythritol
- 1/2 tbsp ground cinnamon
- 1 1/2 tsp espresso grounds
- 2 tsp of baking powder
- 30 drops liquid stevia
- 2 large eggs

For the espresso cookie dip:
- 1/4 cup heavy whipping cream
- 10 drops liquid stevia
- 1 tsp espresso grounds

Preparation Instructions:
1. Preheat the oven to 350 F.
2. Place parchment paper over a baking sheet.
3. Combine the butter, stevia, baking powder, espresso grounds, cinnamon, erythritol, coconut flour, almond flour, and espresso. Whisk together using a hand-held electric mixer.
4. Add the eggs and continue to whisk until completely combined.
5. Scoop out the batter using a spoon and place them onto the baking tray.
6. Put the cookies in the oven and bake for 15 minutes.
7. Once cooked, remove the cookies from the oven and allow them to cool down completely.
8. Make the dip by putting the cream into a small bowl and use an electric mixer to whisk until stiff peaks are formed.
9. Add the espresso grounds and the stevia and continue to whisk together thoroughly.

Macros:
Calories: 123
Fat: 11g
Carbohydrates: 3g
Protein: 2g

128. Coconut Chia Cookies

Preparation time: 10 minutes
Cook time: 8 minutes
Servings: 16

Ingredients:
- 2 eggs
- ½ cup coconut oil
- 3 tbsp chia seeds
- 1 cup coconut flour
- 3 cups ground almonds
- 1 tsp of baking soda
- 2 tsp Swerve
- ½ cup unsweetened cocoa powder
- ½ tsp salt

Preparation Instructions:
1. Add all ingredients to a large bowl and mix until well combined.
2. Roll dough out on a clean surface and cut cookies using a cookie cutter.
3. Spray a spring-form pan with cooking spray. Place cookies in the pan.
4. Pour 2 cups of water into the Instant Pot and place a trivet in the pot.
5. Place pan on top of the trivet.
6. Seal pot with lid and cook on high pressure for 8 minutes.
7. When finished, release pressure using quick release method and open the lid.
8. Serve and enjoy.

Macros:
Calories 187
Fat 17.2 g
Carbohydrates 6.4 g
Protein 5.4 g

129. Almond Scones

Preparation time: 10 minutes
Cook time: 10 minutes
Servings: 6

Ingredients:
- 2 eggs
- ½ cup almond butter, melted
- 1 cup almond flour
- 1 cup fresh strawberries, chopped
- 1 tsp vanilla extract
- 2 tsp of baking powder
- 1 tsp Swerve
- ½ tsp salt

Preparation Instructions:
1. In a large bowl, combine all the dry ingredients.
2. Add vanilla, almond butter, and eggs and beat using a hand mixer until well combined.
3. Add strawberries and stir well.
4. Make six scones from the mixture and place in a baking dish. Set aside.
5. Pour 2 cups of water into the Instant Pot and place a trivet in the pot.
6. Place the baking dish on top of the trivet.
7. Seal pot with lid and cook on high pressure for 10 minutes.
8. When finished, release pressure using quick release method and open the lid.

Macros:
Calories 68
Fat 4.6 g
Carbohydrates 4.4 g
Protein 3.3 g

130. Almond Cinnamon Pancakes

Preparation time: 10 minutes
Cook time: 3 minutes
Servings: 4

Ingredients:

- 4 eggs
- 2 tbsp heavy cream
- 3 tbsp butter
- 3 tsp of baking powder
- 3 tbsp coconut flour
- ¼ cup almond flour
- ¼ tsp nutmeg
- ½ tsp cinnamon
- 2 tsp vanilla extract
- ¼ tsp salt

Preparation Instructions:

1. In a large bowl, add all ingredients and beat using a hand mixer until a smooth batter forms.
2. Spray the Instant Pot inside with cooking spray.
3. Set the Instant Pot on sauté mode.
4. Pour ¼ cup of batter into the pot and cook for 2–3 minutes.
5. Gently remove the pancake from the pot and make the remaining pancakes.

Macros:
Calories 231
Fat 18.2 g
Carbohydrates 9.3 g
Protein 7.7 g

131. Butterscotch Pudding

Preparation time: 10 minutes
Cook time: 18 minutes
Servings: 6

Ingredients:

- 2 tsp. of molasses or yacón syrup
- 1 stick (½ cup) of salted Butter, divided
- ¾ cup of powdered Erythritol-based Sweetener
- 1 cup of heavy Whipping Cream
- 1 tbsp. of Whiskey (optional)
- 1 cup of unsweetened Almond Milk
- 4 large egg yolks
- 1 tsp. of Caramel extract or Butterscotch
- ½ tsp. of Vanilla extract
- ½ tsp. of Xanthan gum

Preparation Instructions:

1. Over medium heat, melt 6 tbsp. of butter for 4 minutes until it appears amber.
2. Add the yacón syrup and sweetener and keep whisking. Slowly add the almond milk and cream and keep whisking. Allow to simmer for a while and remove from heat. If using whiskey, stir it in.
3. Carefully mix a cup of the hot cream mixture with the yolks and keep whisking. Combine the egg mixture with the rest of the cream in the saucepan.
4. Place over medium heat and allow to cook. Keep whisking for 5-10 minutes until the pudding begins to thicken and bubble. Remove the pan from the heat and add the remaining two tbsp. of the extracts and butter and mix it in.
5. Sprinkle the top of the pudding with xanthan gum and quickly resume whisking to thoroughly mix. Scrape the sides and bottom of the pan and keep whisking until it becomes very smooth.
6. Pour the pudding into 5 dessert cups and refrigerate for 3 hours.

132. Dairy-Free Peanut Butter Mousse

Preparation time: 10 minutes
Cook time: 22 mins
Servings: 6

Ingredients:

- 2 tbsp. plus ¼ cup of salted creamy Peanut Butter
- 2 tbsp. of slightly softened Coconut Oil
- ½ tsp. of Vanilla extract
- 1 (13.5 oz.) can of full-fat Coconut Milk, placed in a refrigerator overnight
- ¼ cup of powdered Erythritol-based Sweetener

Preparation Instructions:

1. Beat the coconut oil and peanut butter in a medium bowl using an electric mixer until thoroughly combined.
2. Skim the coconut cream (the solid portion) from the top of the can of coconut milk into the bowl and keep beating until it is well mixed.
3. Beat in the vanilla extract and sweetener.
4. Measure out the mousse into six glasses or dessert cups using a spoon and refrigerate for about two hours.

133. Mascarpone Mousse with Roasted Strawberries

Preparation time: 15 minutes
Cook time: 20 minutes
Servings: 6

Ingredients:

- 2 cups of quartered Strawberries
- 2 tsp. of granulated Erythritol-based Sweetener
- ¼ tsp. of Vanilla extract
- 8 oz. of softened Mascarpone Cheese
- 4 oz. (½ cup) of softened Cream Cheese
- 2 tbsp. plus ¼ cup of powdered Erythritol-based Sweetener, divided
- 1 tsp. of Vanilla extract
- 1 cup of heavy Whipping Cream

Preparation Instructions:

1. Roasting the Strawberries:
2. Heat the oven to 375° F and carefully grease a medium-sized baking dish. Put the strawberries inside the greased dish and trickle with granulated sweetener. Add the vanilla extract and evenly spread it in the pan.
3. For 20 minutes, roast until the berries becomes tender and soft. Prepare the mousse while the berries are roasting.
4. To Make the Mousse and Assemble:
5. Beat the vanilla extract, ¼ cup of ground sweetener, cream cheese, and mascarpone using an electric mixer until it is thoroughly mixed.
6. Beat the cream plus the rest of the ground sweetener in a separate bowl until it holds stiff peaks. Wrap the whipped cream in mascarpone until it is thoroughly mixed.
7. Spoon the mousse into six glasses or desserts cups. Place roasted strawberries on top and serve.

134. Chocolate Hazelnut Mousse

Preparation time: 10 minutes
Cook time: 25 minutes
Servings: 6

Ingredients:

- ½ stick (¼ cup) softened unsalted Butter
- ½ cup of Homemade Chocolate Hazelnut Spread
- ½-⅔ cup heavy Whipping cream, divided
- ⅓ cup of ground erythritol-based Sweetener
- ½ tsp. of vanilla extract or hazelnut

Preparation Instructions:

1. Using an electric mixer, cream the butter in a medium bowl until smooth. Add the sweetener and chocolate hazelnut until thoroughly mixed.
2. Add the hazelnuts and ½ cup of cream and beat until smooth. Add the rest of the cream if the mixture is too thick.
3. Spoon the mousse into six glasses or dessert cups. Serve immediately or refrigerate to chill before serving.

135. Perfect Pumpkin Pudding

Preparation time: 10 minutes
Cook time: 30 minutes
Servings: 6

Ingredients:

- 2 large eggs
- 1 tsp vanilla extract
- 3/4 tsp pumpkin pie spice
- 15 oz pumpkin puree
- ¾ cup Swerve
- ½ cup unsweetened almond milk

Preparation Instructions:

1. Grease a 6-inch baking dish with butter and set aside.
2. In a large bowl, whisk the eggs with the remaining ingredients.
3. Pour mixture into prepared baking dish and cover with foil.
4. Pour 1 ½ cups of water into the instant pot then place a steamer rack in the pot.
5. Place baking dish on top of steamer rack.
6. Seal instant pot with lid and cook on manual high pressure for 20 minutes.
7. Allow to release pressure naturally for 10 minutes then release using the quick release method.
8. Remove baking dish from the pot and let it cool completely then place in refrigerator for 5-6 hours.
9. Serve chilled and enjoy.

Macros:
Calories 55
Fat 2.2 g
Carbohydrates 6.5 g
Protein 3 g

136. Avocado Pudding

Preparation time: 10 minutes
Cook time: 3 minutes
Servings: 2

Ingredients:
- ½ avocado, cut into cubes
- 2 tsp Swerve
- ¼ cup coconut cream
- 1 cup of coconut milk
- 1 tsp vanilla extract
- 1 tsp agar powder

Preparation Instructions:
1. Add coconut cream and avocado to a food processor and process until smooth. Set aside.
2. In a large bowl, combine coconut milk, vanilla, Swerve, and agar powder. Stir until well combined.
3. Add coconut cream and avocado mixture and stir well.
4. Pour mixture into a heat-safe bowl.
5. Pour one cup of water into the Instant Pot and place a trivet in the pot.
6. Place bowl on top of the trivet.
7. Seal pot with lid and select steam mode, and cook for 3 minutes.
8. When finished, release pressure using quick release method and open the lid.
9. Remove bowl from the pot and set aside to cool completely.
10. Place bowl in refrigerator for 1 hour.
11. Serve and enjoy.

Macros:
Calories 245
Fat 23 g
Carbohydrates 9.9 g
Protein 2.4 g

137. Coconut Custard

Preparation time: 10 minutes
Cook time: 40 minutes
Servings: 4

Ingredients:
- 5 eggs
- ¼ cup coconut milk
- 2 tbsp chia seeds
- ½ tsp agar powder
- 2 tbsp Swerve
- 1 cup heavy cream
- ¼ tsp cinnamon
- 1 tsp vanilla extract

Preparation Instructions:
1. In a large bowl, add coconut milk, chia seeds, agar powder, Swerve, eggs, and heavy cream, and beat using a hand mixer until creamy.
2. Stir in vanilla and beat for a minute.
3. Pour custard into ramekins and cover with foil. Set aside.
4. Pour 1 cup of water into the Instant Pot and place a trivet in the pot.
5. Place ramekins on top of the trivet.
6. Seal pot with lid and cook on slow cook mode for 40 minutes.
7. When finished, release pressure using quick release method and open the lid.
8. Remove ramekins from the pot and set aside to cool completely.
9. Place ramekins in the refrigerator for 1 hour.
10. Serve chilled and enjoy.

Macros:
Calories 240
Fat 21.3 g
Carbohydrates 4.1 g
Protein 8.7 g

138. Vanilla egg Custard

Preparation time: 10 minutes
Cook time: 7 minutes
Servings: 6

Ingredients:

- 6 large eggs
- 1 tsp vanilla
- 4 cups cream
- 3/4 cup Swerve
- Pinch of salt

Preparation Instructions:

1. In a large mixing bowl, beat the eggs.
2. Add cream, vanilla, salt, and swerve and blend until well combined.
3. Pour blended mixture into the baking dish and cover with foil.
4. Pour 1 1/2 cups of water into the instant pot then place a trivet in the pot.
5. Place baking dish on top of the trivet.
6. Seal pot with lid and cook on high pressure for 7 minutes.
7. Allow to release pressure naturally for 10 minutes then release using the quick release method.
8. Serve and enjoy.

Macros:

Calories 168
Fat 13.3 g
Carbohydrates 5.7 g
Protein 6.8 g

139. Choco Almond Fudge

Preparation time: 10 minutes
Cook time: 15 minutes
Servings: 8

Ingredients:

- 5 eggs
- ½ cup unsweetened almond milk
- 2 tsp Swerve
- ½ cup cocoa powder
- ½ cup unsweetened dark chocolate
- 2 cups almond flour
- 1 tsp vanilla extract
- 1 tsp of baking soda
- 1 tsp of baking powder
- ½ tsp salt

Preparation Instructions:

1. Add all dry ingredients to a large bowl and mix until well combined.
2. Add remaining ingredients and beat using a hand mixer until well mixed.
3. Pour 2 cups of water into the Instant Pot and place a trivet in the pot.
4. Pour batter into a pan and place pan on top of the trivet.
5. Seal pot with lid and cook on steam mode for 15 minutes.
6. When finished, release pressure using quick release method, and then open the lid. Remove the pan and allow to cool.
7. Serve and enjoy.

Macros:

Calories 197
Fat 15.2 g
Carbohydrates 9.7 g
Protein 8 g

140. Almond Berry Mousse

Preparation time: 10 minutes
Cook time: 10 minutes
Servings: 4

Ingredients:

- 4 blueberries
- 4 strawberries, sliced
- ½ cup heavy cream
- 2 egg yolks
- ½ tsp vanilla extract
- ¼ cup almond milk
- ¼ cup Swerve
- 2 tbsp water

Preparation Instructions:

1. Pour 1½ cups of water into the Instant Pot and place a trivet in the pot.
2. In a small saucepan, add sweetener and 2 tbsp. water and heat over medium heat until sweetener is dissolved.
3. Remove pan from heat and whisk in vanilla, milk, and cream.
4. In a bowl, whisk egg yolks.
5. Slowly add cream mixture and stir into the eggs.
6. Pour mixture into 4 ramekins and place on top of the trivet.
7. Seal pot with lid and cook on high pressure for 6 minutes.
8. When finished, release pressure using quick release method and open the lid.
9. Remove ramekins from the pot and set aside to cool completely.
10. Place in refrigerator for 1–2 hours.
11. Top with blueberries and sliced strawberries and serve. You can use any of favorite berries.

Macros:

Calories 125
Fat 7.8 g
Carbohydrates 13 g
Protein 2.5 g

141. Lime, Avocado and Rhubarb Mousse

Preparation time: 10 minutes
Cook time: 0 minutes
Servings: 2

Ingredients:

- ½ cup avocado, peeled, pitted and mashed
- 1 cup rhubarb, chopped
- 1 tsp vanilla extract
- 1 cup coconut cream
- 1 tsp lime juice
- 2 tbsp. stevia

Preparation Instructions:

In a blender, mix the ingredients, pulse well, divide into cups and keep in the fridge before serving.

Macros: Calories 122, fat 5.7, fiber 3.2, carbs 5.3, protein 0.4

142. Cocoa, Avocado and Mint Mousse

Preparation time: 10 minutes
Cook time: 0 minutes
Servings: 4
Ingredients:
- ½ cup cocoa powder
- ¾ cup almond milk
- 1 cup avocado, peeled, pitted and mashed
- ¼ cup stevia
- 1 tsp mint, dried
- 1 tsp vanilla extract

Preparation Instructions:
In a blender, mix the ingredients, pulse well, divide into cups and serve cold.
Macros: Calories 162, fat 3.4, fiber 2.4, carbs 5, protein 1

143. Simple Strawberry Mousse

Preparation time: 10 minutes
Cook time: 0 minutes
Servings: 4
Ingredients:
- 1 cup strawberries, chopped
- 1 cup coconut cream
- 1 tbsp stevia
- 1 tsp lime juice
- ½ tsp vanilla extract

Preparation Instructions:
In a blender, combine ingredients, pulse well, divide into cups and serve cold.
Macros: Calories 182, fat 3.1, fiber 2.3, carbs 3.5, protein 2

144. Date, Avocado and Cherry Mousse

Preparation time: 2 hours
Cook time: 0 minutes
Servings: 6
Ingredients:
- 2 tbsp. ghee, melted
- 1 cup dates, chopped
- 1 avocado, peeled, pitted and mashed
- ½ cup cherries, pitted
- 1 cup coconut cream
- 1 tsp almond extract
- 3 tbsp. stevia

Preparation Instructions:
In a blender, mix the ingredients, pulse well, divide into cups and keep in the fridge for 2 hours before serving.
Macros: Calories 141, fat 10.2, fiber 2.4, carbs 13.8, protein 1.4

145. Cherries and Peach Mousse

Preparation time: 10 minutes
Cook time: 0 minutes
Servings: 4

Ingredients:
- 1 cup cherries, pitted and halved
- 1 cup peach, chopped
- ½ cup coconut milk
- ½ tsp gelatin powder
- ¼ cup coconut cream
- 2 tbsp. stevia
- 1 tsp vanilla extract

Preparation Instructions:
In a blender, mix the cherries with the peach, milk and other ingredients, pulse well, divide into bowls and serve cold.

Macros: Calories 122, fat 4, fiber 5.3, carbs 6.6, protein 4.5

146. Avocado and Peach Mousse

Preparation time: 10 minutes
Cook time: 0 minutes
Servings: 4

Ingredients:
- 2 cups heavy cream
- 1 cup avocado, peeled, pitted and mashed
- 1 cup peach, chopped
- 2 tbsp. stevia
- Zest of 1 lime, grated
- 1 tbsp. lime juice

Preparation Instructions:
In a blender, mix the ingredients, pulse well, divide into cups and serve cold.

Macros: Calories 172, fat 5.6, fiber 3.5, carbs 7.6, protein 4

147. Cinnamon Avocado Mousse

Preparation time: 5 minutes
Cook time: 0 minutes
Servings: 4

Ingredients:
- 1 cup avocado, peeled, pitted and mashed
- 1 cup heavy cream
- 1 cup coconut cream
- 1 tsp cinnamon powder
- 4 tbsp. stevia

Preparation Instructions:
In a blender, mix the ingredients, pulse well, divide into bowls and serve cold.

Macros: Calories 162, fat 8, fiber 4.2, carbs 12.3, protein 8.4

148. Berry, Lime and Almond Mousse

Preparation time: 5 minutes
Cook time: 0 minutes
Servings: 4

Ingredients:

- 1 cup heavy cream
- 1 tbsp blackberries
- 1 tbsp blueberries
- Juice of 1 lime
- ½ cup coconut cream
- 3 tbsp. stevia
- 1 tsp almond extract

Preparation Instructions:

1. In a blender, mix the heavy cream with coconut cream, stevia, almond extract and lime juice, pulse well and divide into cups.
2. Sprinkle the berries on top of each serving and cool down before serving.

Macros: Calories 192, fat 6.5, fiber 3.4, carbs 9.5, protein 5

149. Green Tea Mousse

Preparation time: 10 minutes
Cook time: 0 minutes
Servings: 4

Ingredients:

- ¼ tbsp green tea powder
- 1 cup heavy cream
- ½ cup almond milk
- 2 tbsp. stevia
- 1 tsp vanilla extract
- 1 tsp almond extract

Preparation Instructions:

In a blender, combine the ingredients, pulse well, divide into bowls and serve cold.

Macros: Calories 300, fat 30.8, fiber 0, carbs 3, protein 4

150. Peach, Avocado and Cinnamon Mousse

Preparation time: 10 minutes
Cook time: 0 minutes
Servings: 4

Ingredients:

- 2 cups heavy cream
- 1 cup peach, chopped
- ½ cup avocado, peeled, pitted and mashed
- 1 tsp cinnamon powder
- 2 tbsp. stevia
- 1 tsp vanilla extract

Preparation Instructions:

In a blender, mix the ingredients, pulse well, divide into bowls and serve cold.

Macros: Calories 346, fat 35.5, fiber 0, carbs 3.4, protein 4.6

151. Cream Cheese, Avocado and Coconut Mousse

Preparation time: 30 minutes
Cook time: minutes
Servings: 4
Ingredients:

- 1 tsp vanilla extract
- 1 cup avocado, peeled, pitted and mashed
- 1 cup coconut flesh, unsweetened and shredded
- ½ cup cream cheese, soft
- 1 cup coconut cream
- 2 tbsp. stevia

Preparation Instructions:
In a blender, mix the ingredients, pulse well, divide into bowls and keep in the fridge for 30 minutes before serving.
Macros: Calories 329, fat 32.7, fiber 0, carbs 2.5, protein 5.7

152. Chocolate Coconut Mousse

Preparation time: 10 minutes
Cook time: 0 minutes
Servings: 6
Ingredients:

- 2 cups coconut cream
- ½ cup coconut flakes, unsweetened
- 1 cup dark chocolate, melted
- 1 tsp vanilla extract
- 1 tbsp stevia

Preparation Instructions:
In a blender, mix the ingredients, pulse well, divide into bowls and serve cold.
Macros: Calories 359, fat 29.6, fiber 3.3, carbs 22.2, protein 4.2

153. Chocolate Watermelon Mousse

Preparation time: 2 hours
Cook time: 0 minutes
Servings: 6
Ingredients:

- 2 cups watermelon, peeled and cubed
- ½ cup dark chocolate, unsweetened
- 1 tbsp stevia
- 1 cup coconut cream
- 1 tsp vanilla extract

Preparation Instructions:
In a blender, combine the ingredients, pulse well, divide into cups and keep in the fridge for 2 hours before serving.
Macros: Calories 184, fat 13.6, fiber 1.6, carbs 14.4, protein 2.3

154. Ginger Mousse

Preparation time: 10 minutes
Cook time: 0 minutes
Servings: 4
Ingredients:
- 2 tbsp. stevia
- 2 tbsp. ginger, grated
- 2 cups coconut cream
- 1 tsp vanilla extract
- 1 tsp almond extract
- ¼ tsp gelatin powder mixed with 1 tsp water

Preparation Instructions:
In a blender, combine the ingredients, pulse well, divide into bowls and serve cold.
Macros: Calories 291, fat 28.8, fiber 3, carbs 8.8, protein 3

155. Mint and Ginger Chocolate Mousse

Preparation time: 20 minutes
Cook time: 0 minutes
Servings: 6
Ingredients:
- 1 cup coconut cream
- 1 cup heavy cream
- ¼ cup almond milk
- 1 tsp mint, dried
- 1 tsp ginger powder
- 4 tbsp. cocoa powder
- 1 tsp vanilla extract
- 4 tbsp. stevia

Preparation Instructions:
In a blender, mix the ingredients, pulse well, divide into bowls and keep in the fridge for 20 minutes before serving.
Macros: Calories 195, fat 19.8, fiber 2.2, carbs 5.6, protein 2.3

156. Berry Chia Pudding

Preparation time: 10 minutes
Cook time: 20 minutes
Servings: 1
Ingredients
- ½ cup berries, fresh
- 8 tbsp. chia seeds
- 1 tbsp coconut flakes
- 1 tsp erythritol sweetener
- 2 tbsp. whey protein powder
- 1/8 tsp sea salt
- 2 tbsp. MCT oil
- 3 cups coconut milk, unsweetened, full-fat

Preparation Instructions:
1. Place berries in a bowl, pour in milk, add oil and protein powder, sprinkle with salt and sweetener and blend using an immersion blender until smooth.
2. Place chia seeds in a serving bowl, top with berries mixture and stir well.
3. Refrigerate the pudding for a minimum of 4 hours, then garnish with coconut flakes and serve.
Macros:461.2 Calories; 43 g Fats; 6.7 g Protein; 9 g Net Carb; 3 g Fiber

157. Peanut Butter Chia Pudding

Preparation time: 10 minutes
Cook time: 20 minutes
Servings: 6
Ingredients
For the Pudding:
- 1/4 cup ground chia seeds
- 1/4 tsp sea salt
- 1 tsp vanilla essence, unsweetened
- 1/4 cup liquid stevia
- 1 cup peanut butter, unsweetened
- 1 1/4 cup almond milk, unsweetened

For the Topping:
- 1 tsp peanut butter, unsweetened
- 1/2 tsp crushed peanuts
- 1 tsp melted dark chocolate, stevia-sweetened
- 1 tsp dark chocolate chunks, stevia-sweetened
- ½ cup sliced strawberries

Preparation Instructions:
1.   Place all the ingredients for the pudding in a food processor or blender and pulse for 1 minute or until smooth and creamy.
2.   Evenly divide the pudding into six small glass jars, cover with their lid and refrigerate for a minimum of 3 hours.
3.   Then top the pudding with peanut butter, berries, peanuts and chocolate and serve.
Macros: 330 Calories; 28 g Fats; 9.3 g Protein; 10 g Net Carb; 4.9 g Fiber

158. Matcha Chia Seed Pudding

Preparation time: 4 hours
Cook time: 15 minutes
Servings: 4
Ingredients
- 1/3 cup chia seeds
- 1 tbsp erythritol sweetener
- 2 scoops Matcha MCT powder
- 1/2 cup whipped heavy cream, grass-fed, full-fat
- 1 1/2 cups almond milk, unsweetened

Preparation Instructions:
1.   Place all the ingredients in a large bowl and stir well until mixed.
2.   Cover the bowl with lid and refrigerate for a minimum of 4 hours or until pudding is thick.
3.   Top the pudding with cream and serve.
Macros: 110 Calories; 19 g Fats; 3 g Protein; 2 g Net Carb; 5 g Fiber

159. Vanilla Chia Seed Pudding

Preparation time: 4 hours
Cook time: 15 minutes
Servings: 4

Ingredients

- 1/3 cup chia seeds
- 4 tbsp. erythritol sweetener
- 2 tsp. vanilla extract, unsweetened
- 1/8 tsp salt
- 1/2 cup heavy cream, grass-fed, full-fat
- 1 cup coconut milk, full-fat, unsweetened

Preparation Instructions:

Place all the ingredients in a food processor or blender and pulse until well blended.

Tip the pudding in a bowl, stir it again, then cover the bowl and refrigerate for a minimum of 4 hours or until pudding is thick.

Macros: 288 Calories; 27 g Fats; 4 g Protein; 4 g Net Carb; 4 g Fiber

160. Vanilla Pudding

Preparation time: 10 minutes
Cook time: 20 minutes
Servings: 6

Ingredients

- 1 tbsp cornstarch
- 1/16 tsp salt
- 1/3 cup Swerve sweetener
- 2 eggs, pastured
- 1 cup heavy cream, grass-fed, full-fat
- 3 egg yolks, pastured
- 1/2 cup almond milk, unsweetened, full-fat
- 3/4 tsp gelatin powder, grass-fed
- 1 tsp vanilla extract, unsweetened
- 2 tbsp. butter, unsalted
- 1/4 tsp stevia sweetener
- 1 tbsp water

Preparation Instructions:

1. Place a small pot over medium heat, add cream, then whisk in milk until combined and bring the mixture to boil.
2. Meanwhile, place water in a bowl, sprinkle with gelatin and set aside until required.
3. Then place cornstarch in a heatproof bowl, add salt and Swerve sweetener and whisk well.
4. Whisk in eggs and egg yolks until blended and then slowly whisk in the hot creamy mixture until incorporated.
5. Return mixture to the pot, heat it over medium-low heat and continue cooking for 5 minutes or until thickened, whisking continuously.
6. Switch heat to low, continue whisking the pudding for 2 minutes, then remove the pot from the heat and whisk the pudding for 1 minute.
7. Pass the pudding through a sieve placed over a bowl, then add butter into the collected pudding in the bowl along with stevia and vanilla and whisk well.
8. Whisk in gelatin until incorporated, cover the pudding with plastic wrap, pushing the wrap down onto the surface of the pudding and refrigerate for 8 hours or until chilled and firm.
9. Whip the chilled pudding with an immersion blender and serve.

Macros: 235 Calories; 23 g Fats; 4 g Protein; 3 g Net Carb; 0 g Fiber

161. Chocolate Pudding

Preparation time: 10 minutes
Cook time: 20 minutes
Servings: 4

Ingredients
- 2 cups heavy cream, grass-fed, full-fat, divided
- 1/4 cup cocoa powder, unsweetened
- 1/3 cup powdered erythritol sweetener
- 1/4 tsp sea salt
- 1 1/2 tsp gelatin powder, grass-fed
- 2 tsp. vanilla extract, unsweetened

Preparation Instructions:
1. Place ¼ cup of heavy cream in a bowl, sprinkle gelatin on top, then whisk well and set aside.
2. Pour remaining cream in a saucepan, place it over medium-low heat, add sweetener, salt, and cocoa powder, whisk well and cook for 5 minutes or until smooth and mixture starts to bubble.
3. Remove the saucepan from heat, stir in vanilla, then add gelatin mixture and whisk well until gelatin has dissolved.
4. Let the pudding rest at room temp for 10 minutes or until slightly cooled and then whisk again.
5. Cover the pudding with plastic wrap, pushing the wrap down onto the surface of the pudding and then refrigerate for 2 hours or until chilled and firm.

Macros: 431 Calories; 43 g Fats; 5 g Protein; 5 g Net Carb; 6 g Fiber

162. Almond Butter Mousse with Strawberries

Preparation time: 10 minutes
Cook time: 20 minutes
Servings: 1

Ingredients
- 1/2 cup strawberries, fresh
- 1/8 tsp cinnamon
- 4 tbsp. almond butter, unsweetened
- 1/4 tsp vanilla extract, unsweetened
- 2 tbsp stevia sweetener
- 1 cup almond milk, full-fat, unsweetened

Preparation Instructions:
1. Place all the ingredients in a saucepan except for berries and then blend using an immersion blender until smooth.
2. Place the saucepan over medium heat, bring the mixture to a gentle boil and continue simmering for 8 to 10 minutes.
3. Then remove the saucepan from heat and let the pudding cool to room temp.
4. Line a small serving dish with strawberries, then drizzle with cooled mousse and more layers in the same manner.

Macros: 167 Calories; 16 g Fats; 3 g Protein; 1 g Net Carb; 0 g Fiber

163. Raspberry Cheesecake Mousse

Preparation time: 10 minutes
Cook time: 20 minutes
Servings: 15

Ingredients

- 1 cup raspberries, fresh
- 1 tsp vanilla extract, unsweetened
- 1/2 cup Swerve confectioners
- 8 oz. cream cheese, grass-fed, full-fat, softened
- 1 cup heavy cream, grass-fed, full-fat

Preparation Instructions:

1. Place cream cheese in a bowl and beat using an immersion blender until smooth.
2. Blend in the berries until combined and then whisk in heavy cream until whipped.
3. Add vanilla and stevia and then blend until well combined.

Macros: 275 Calories; 26 g Fats; 2 g Protein; 3 g Net Carb; 1 g Fiber

164. Chocolate Mascarpone Mousse

Preparation time: 10 minutes
Cook time: 20 minutes
Servings: 15

Ingredients

For the Chocolate Mascarpone Mousse:

- 8.8 oz. mascarpone, grass-fed, full-fat
- 4 tbsp. cocoa powder, unsweetened
- 4 tbsp. powdered erythritol sweetener
- 8.8 oz. heavy cream, grass-fed, full-fat

For the Vanilla Mousse:

- 2 tbsp. powdered erythritol sweetener
- 1 tsp vanilla extract, unsweetened
- 3.5 oz. cream cheese, grass-fed, full-fat
- 3.5 oz. heavy cream, grass-fed, full-fat

Preparation Instructions:

1. To prepare the Mascarpone mousse, place ingredients in a bowl and whisk using an immersion blender until creamy.
2. Prepare the vanilla mousse and for this, place heavy cream in a bowl, whisk until whipped and then whisk in vanilla, cream cheese, and sweetener until well combined.
3. Assemble the mouse and for this, evenly divide the Mascarpone mousse between eight serving glasses, top with a dollop of the prepared vanilla mousse and then swirl with a fork or knife to create marble effect in the mousse.
4. Refrigerate the mousse for 1 hour and serve.

Macros: 338 Calories; 35 g Fats; 2 g Protein; 3.2 g Net Carb; 1.1 g Fiber

165. Berry Mousse

Preparation time: 10 minutes
Cook time: 20 minutes
Servings: 8

Ingredients

- 2 oz. chopped pecans
- 3 oz. raspberries, fresh
- ½ lemon, zested
- ¼ tsp vanilla extract, unsweetened
- 2 cups heavy whipping cream, grass-fed, full-fat

Preparation Instructions:

1. Place the heavy cream in a bowl, then whisk with an immersion blender until soft peaks form and then whisk in vanilla and lemon zest until combined.
2. Stir in pecans and berries until well mixed, then cover the bowl with plastic wrap and refrigerate for 3 hours or until the mousse has firmed.

Macros :255 Calories; 26 g Fats; 2 g Protein; 3 g Net Carb; 1 g Fiber

166. Peanut Butter Mousse

Preparation time: 10 minutes
Cook time: 20 minutes
Servings: 4

Ingredients

- 1/4 cup powdered Swerve Sweetener
- ½ tsp vanilla extract, unsweetened
- 1/4 cup peanut butter, unsweetened
- 4 oz. cream cheese, grass-fed, full-fat, softened
- ½ cup heavy whipping cream, grass-fed, full-fat

Preparation Instructions:

1. Place heavy cream in a bowl and whisk with an immersion blender until stiff peaks form, set aside until required.
2. Place cream cheese in another bowl, add butter and then whisk with an immersion blender until creamy and smooth.
3. Beat in vanilla and sweetener until mixed and then fold in heavy cream mixture until combined.

Macros: 301 Calories; 26.5 g Fats; 6 g Protein; 4.8 g Net Carb; 0.8 g Fiber

167. Cheesecake Mousse

Preparation time: 10 minutes
Cook time: 20 minutes
Servings: 6

Ingredients

- 8 oz. cream cheese, grass-fed, full-fat, softened
- 1/3 cup powdered erythritol sweetener
- 1/8 tsp powdered stevia sweetener
- 1 1/2 tsp. vanilla extract, unsweetened
- 1/4 tsp lemon extract, unsweetened
- 1 cup heavy whipping cream, grass-fed, full-fat

Preparation Instructions:

1. Place heavy cream in a bowl and whisk with an immersion blender until stiff peaks form.
2. Place cream cheese in another bowl, whisk with an immersion blender until smooth, then add sweeteners, lemon extract and vanilla and whisk until well combined.
3. Fold in half of the heavy cream until well incorporated, then fold in the other half of the cream and beat until light and fluffy.
4. Place the mousse in the refrigerator for 2 hours and serve.

Macros: 269 Calories; 27 g Fats; 3 g Protein; 2 g Net Carb; 0 g Fiber

ICE CREAM

168. Milk and egg Ice Cream

Preparation time: 10 hours
Cook time: 10 minutes
Servings: 8
Ingredients:
- 2 cups coconut cream
- 1 cup coconut milk
- 3 tbsp. stevia
- 5 egg yolks, whisked
- 1 tsp vanilla extract

Preparation Instructions:
1. Put the milk in a pot, heat over medium heat, add the cream and the other ingredients, whisk well and cook for 10 minutes.
2. Remove from heat, cool down, transfer to a container and freeze for 10 hours before serving.

Macros: Calories 400, fat 12, fiber 3, carbs 34, protein 2

169. Hazelnut Ice Cream

Preparation time: 6 hours
Cook time: 0 minutes
Servings: 6
Ingredients:
- 1 cup hazelnuts, chopped
- 1 cup coconut cream
- 12 oz. almond milk
- 1 tsp vanilla extract
- 1 tsp almond extract

Preparation Instructions:
In a blender, combine the ingredients, pulse well, transfer to a container and freeze for 6 hours before serving.

Macros: Calories 400, fat 16, fiber 3, carbs 18, protein 4

170. Hazelnut and Cocoa Ice Cream

Preparation time: 10 hours
Cook time: 10 minutes
Servings: 12
Ingredients:
- 8 egg yolks
- 1 cup almond milk
- 1 cup heavy cream
- 3 tbsp. stevia
- ½ cup hazelnuts, chopped
- 1 tbsp gelatin powder
- 3 tsp. vanilla extract

Preparation Instructions:
1. In a pot, combine the egg yolks with the milk and other ingredients, whisk, and cook for 10 minutes.
2. Remove from heat, cool down and keep in the fridge for 8 hours.
3. Pour into ice cream maker, process, transfer to a container and freeze for 2 hours before serving.

Macros: Calories 300, fat 22, fiber 2, carbs 18, protein 5

171. Hazelnut and Cherry Ice Cream

Preparation time: 4 hours
Cook time: 10 minutes
Servings: 8
Ingredients:
- 2 cups hazelnuts, chopped
- 1 cup cherries, pitted and halved
- 1 cup almond milk
- 1 cup coconut cream
- 3 tbsp. stevia
- 2 eggs, whisked

Preparation Instructions:
1. In a blender, combine the hazelnuts with the cherries, milk and other ingredients, whisk and transfer to a pot.
2. Heat over medium heat for 10 minutes, transfer to a container and freeze for 4 hours before serving.

Macros: Calories 400, fat 23, fiber 2, carbs 12, protein 22

172. Almond Raspberry Ice Cream

Preparation time: 4 hours
Cook time: 10 minutes
Servings: 10
Ingredients:
- 1 cup heavy cream
- 1 cup almond milk
- 1 cup raspberries
- 2 eggs, whisked
- 1 tsp almond extract
- 3 tbsp. stevia
- 2/3 cup almonds, chopped

Preparation Instructions:
1. In a pot, combine the cream with milk, raspberries and the other ingredients, whisk and simmer over medium heat for 10 minutes.
2. Remove from heat, cool down, transfer to a container and chill for 4 hours before serving.

Macros: Calories 400, fat 23, fiber 4, carbs 11, protein 3

173. Date and Almonds Ice Cream

Preparation time: 4 hours
Cook time: 15 minutes
Servings: 12
Ingredients:
- 14 oz. coconut milk
- 1 cup almonds, chopped
- ½ cup dates, pitted
- 1 tbsp vanilla extract
- ¼ tsp almond extract

Preparation Instructions:
1. Arrange the almonds on a lined baking sheet, place in the oven at 350 F, toast for 15 minutes, transfer to a bowl and crush them.
2. Add the rest of the ingredients, whisk well, transfer everything to a container and freeze for 4 hours before serving.

Macros: Calories 400, fat 13, fiber 2, carbs 27, protein 1

174. Strawberry and Chia Ice Cream

Preparation time: 4 hours
Cook time: 10 minutes
Servings: 8
Ingredients:
- 1 cup coconut cream
- 1 cup coconut milk
- ½ cup strawberries, chopped
- 2 tbsp. chia seeds
- 1 tbsp water
- 1 and ½ tsp. gelatin powder
- 1 tsp vanilla extract

Preparation Instructions:
1.   In a pot, combine the cream with the berries, chia and the other ingredients, toss and simmer for 10 minutes over medium heat.
2.   Remove from heat, cool down, transfer to a blender and pulse well.
3.   Transfer this to ice cream maker, process according to instructions, put the ice cream in the freezer for 4 hours and serve.

Macros: Calories 370, fat 11, fiber 3, carbs 22, protein 4

175. Cinnamon Walnut Ice Cream

Preparation time: 4 hours
Cook time: 10 minutes
Servings: 8
Ingredients:
- 1 tsp gelatin powder
- 1 cup coconut cream
- 2 ½ cups almond milk
- ½ cup walnuts, toasted and chopped
- 3 tbsp. stevia
- ½ tsp cinnamon, ground

Preparation Instructions:
1.   In a pot, combine the cream with the gelatin and the other ingredients, whisk and heat over medium heat for 10 minutes.
2.   Take this off heat, transfer to a container and keep in the fridge for 3 hours.
3.   Transfer to ice cream maker, process and then freeze for 1 more hour before serving.

Macros: Calories 360, fat 12, fiber 3, carbs 22, protein 3

176. Nutmeg Avocado Ice Cream

Preparation time: 4 hours
Cook time: 0 minutes
Servings: 8
Ingredients:
- ¾ cup walnuts, chopped
- 1 tsp nutmeg, ground
- 1 cup coconut cream
- 20 oz. coconut milk
- 2 tbsp. stevia
- 1 tbsp vanilla extract

Preparation Instructions:
1.   In a blender, combine the walnuts with the cream, nutmeg and the other ingredients and pulse well.
2.   Keep in the fridge for 2 hours, transfer to ice cream maker, process according to instructions and freeze for 2 more hours before serving.

Macros: Calories 389, fat 22, fiber 2, carbs 17, protein 2

177. Almond Butter Ice Cream

Preparation time: 4 hours
Cook time: 0 minutes
Servings: 6

Ingredients:

- 1 cup almond milk
- 1 cup coconut cream
- 1 cup almond butter, soft
- 1 tsp vanilla extract
- 2 tbsp. stevia

Preparation Instructions:

In a blender, combine the ingredients, pulse well, transfer to a container and freeze for 4 hours before serving.

Macros: Calories 250, fat 10, fiber 4, carbs 11, protein 5

178. Pecan Ice Cream

Preparation time: 10 hours
Cook time: 10 minutes
Servings: 8

Ingredients:

- 1 tsp vanilla extract
- 1 cup pecans, toasted and chopped
- 1 cup coconut cream
- 1 cup coconut milk
- 3 tbsp. stevia
- 1 tsp gelatin powder

Preparation Instructions:

1. In a pot, combine the ingredients, whisk and simmer over medium heat for 10 minutes.
2. Cool the mix down and keep in the fridge for 6 hours.
3. Put this into ice cream maker, process and then freeze for 4 hours before serving.

Macros: Calories 400, fat 22, fiber 2, carbs 25, protein 5

179. Hemp Seed Ice Cream

Preparation time: 3 hours
Cook time: 10 minutes
Servings: 8

Ingredients:

- 3 tbsp. stevia
- 3 tbsp. hemp seeds
- ½ tsp vanilla extract
- 2 cups almond milk
- 1 cup coconut milk
- 2 eggs, whisked
- 1 tsp gelatin powder

Preparation Instructions:

1. In a pot, combine the ingredients, stir and place over medium heat for 10 minutes.
2. Cool down, transfer to a container and freeze for 3 hours before serving.

Macros: Calories 320, fat 22, fiber 2, carbs 25, protein 2

180. Creamy Spiced Ice Cream

Preparation time: 4 hours and 20 minutes
Cook time: 10 minutes
Servings: 8
Ingredients:
- ¼ tsp vanilla extract 1 cup almond milk
- 1 cup coconut cream
- ½ tsp nutmeg, ground
- ½ tsp cinnamon powder
- 1 cup walnuts, chopped
- 1 tsp almond extract

Preparation Instructions:
1. In a pot, combine the ingredients, whisk and simmer over medium heat for 10 minutes.
2. Remove from heat and keep the mix in the fridge for 2 hours.
3. Transfer to ice cream maker, process for 20 minutes and freeze ice cream for 2 hours before serving.

Macros: Calories 340, fat 22, fiber 5, carbs 17, protein 6

181. Blueberry and Lime Ice Cream

Preparation time: 4 hours and 10 minutes
Cook time: 0 minutes
Servings: 8
Ingredients:
- 1 tsp gelatin powder
- 2 cups almond milk
- 1 cup blueberries
- Juice of 1 lime
- 3 tbsp. stevia
- 1 tsp vanilla extract

Preparation Instructions:
1. In a blender, combine the milk with the berries and the other ingredients and pulse well.
2. Transfer this to a bowl, cover and chill for 2 hours.
3. Transfer to ice cream maker, process for 10 minutes and freeze for 2 hours before serving.

Macros: Calories 390, fat 21, fiber 3, carbs 22, protein 3

182. Mint and Lime Ice Cream

Preparation time: 3 hours
Cook time: 0 minutes
Servings: 8
Ingredients:
- ½ cup mint leaves
- 2 cups almond milk
- 2 tbsp. stevia
- Juice of 1 lime
- 1 tbsp lime zest, grated
- 1 tsp gelatin powder
- ¼ cup heavy cream

Preparation Instructions:
In a blender, combine the ingredients, pulse well, transfer to a container and freeze for 3 hours before serving.

Macros: Calories 289, fat 8, fiber 2, carbs 9, protein 4

183. Mint Coffee Ice Cream

Preparation time: 3 hours
Cook time: 0 minutes
Servings: 6

Ingredients:
- ¼ cup brewed coffee
- 1 cup coconut milk
- ½ cup coconut cream
- 1 tsp gelatin powder
- 3 tbsp. stevia
- 1 tsp mint, dried
- 1 tsp cinnamon powder

Preparation Instructions:
In a blender, combine the ingredients, pulse well, transfer to ice cream maker, process according to instructions and freeze for 3 hours before serving.

Macros: Calories 230, fat 9, fiber 3, carbs 16, protein 3

184. Raspberry and Vanilla Ice Cream

Preparation time: 4 hours
Cook time: 0 minutes
Servings: 10

Ingredients:
- 1 cup coconut cream
- 1 tsp gelatin powder
- 1 tbsp lime zest, grated
- 2 cups raspberries
- 2 tsp. vanilla extract

Preparation Instructions:
1. In a blender, combine the ingredients, pulse well, transfer to ice cream maker and process according to instructions.
2. Freeze ice cream for at least 4 hours before serving.

Macros: Calories 230, fat 16, fiber 6, carbs 19, protein 3

185. Lemon Rhubarb Ice Cream

Preparation time: 4 hours and 10 minutes
Cook time: 0 minutes
Servings: 8

Ingredients:
- 3 cups rhubarb, sliced
- 1 cup almond milk
- 1 cup coconut cream
- 1 tsp gelatin powder
- 1 tsp lemon juice
- 3 tbsp. stevia

Preparation Instructions:
1. In a blender, combine the ingredients, pulse well, transfer everything to ice cream maker and process according to instructions.
2. Freeze ice cream for at least 4 hours before serving.

Macros: Calories 373, fat 13, fiber 2, carbs 18, protein 2

186. Creamy Watermelon Ice Cream

Preparation time: 3 hours
Cook time: 0 minutes
Servings: 10

Ingredients:

- 2 cups watermelon, peeled, seeds removed and cubed
- 2 tbsp. stevia
- 1 tsp gelatin powder
- 1 cup almond milk
- 1 cup coconut cream
- 1 tsp vanilla extract

Preparation Instructions:

1. In a blender, combine the ingredients and pulse well.
2. Transfer to ice cream maker, process according to instructions and freeze for 3 hours before serving.

Macros: Calories 254, fat 14, fiber 1, carbs 25, protein 3

FAT BOMBS

187. Almond Raspberry Fat Bombs

Preparation time: 1 hour
Cook time: 0 minutes
Servings: 16
Ingredients:
- 2 cups raspberries
- 4 tbsp. almonds, chopped
- ½ cup almond butter, soft
- ¼ cup ghee, melted
- 1 tbsp lemon juice
- 1 tsp vanilla extract
- ½ cup swerve

Preparation Instructions:
1. In blender, combine the ingredients and pulse well.
2. Divide into round molds and freeze for 1 hour before serving.

Macros: Calories 121, fat 14, fiber 2, carbs 4, sugars 1, protein 2.2

188. Acai Berry Bomb

Preparation time: 2 hours
Cook time: 0 minutes
Servings: 12
Ingredients:
- 1 cup acai berries, powdered
- 3 tbsp. ghee, melted
- 2 tbsp. cocoa powder
- 2 tbsp. stevia
- ½ cup almond butter, melted

Preparation Instructions:
1. In blender, mix the ingredients and pulse well.
2. Form small balls, arrange them on a lined baking sheet and freeze for 2 hours before serving.

Macros: Calories 151, fat 12, fiber 1, carbs 2, sugars 1, protein 2

189. Dates and Chocolate Bombs

Preparation time: 2 hours
Cook time: 0 minutes
Servings: 12
Ingredients:
- ½ cup coconut cream
- ½ cup dates, chopped
- ¼ cup ghee, melted
- 2 cups dark chocolate, unsweetened and melted
- 1 tsp lemon zest, grated
- ½ tsp vanilla extract

Preparation Instructions:
1. In a blender, combine the cream with the dates, ghee and the other ingredients and pulse well.
2. Shape round balls out of this mix, arrange them on a lined baking tray and freeze for 2 hours before serving.

Macros: Calories 151, fat 12, fiber 1, carbs 2, sugars 0.4, protein 2

190. Ginger and Avocado Bombs

Preparation time: 2 hours
Cook time: 0 minutes
Servings: 20
Ingredients:
- ½ cup walnuts, chopped
- 1/3 cup ghee, melted
- 1 cup almonds, chopped
- 1 cup avocado, peeled, pitted and mashed
- 3 tbsp. swerve
- 1 tbsp cold water
- 1 tsp ginger, grated

Preparation Instructions:
1. In a food processor, combine the walnuts with the ghee, almonds and the other ingredients and pulse well.
2. Shape medium balls out of this mix, arrange them on a platter and keep in the fridge for 2 hours serving.

Macros: Calories 141, fat 11, fiber 2, carbs 1, sugars 0, protein 2

191. Almond, Cocoa and Dates Bombs

Preparation time: 1 hour
Cook time: 0 minutes
Servings: 20
Ingredients:
- 1 cup almond butter, melted
- 2 tbsp. cocoa powder
- 1 cup dates, chopped
- 1 cup ghee, melted
- ½ tbsp lime zest, grated
- ¼ cup almond flour

Preparation Instructions:
1. In a bowl, mix the ingredients and pulse well.
2. Shape medium balls out of this mix, arrange them on a lined baking sheet and freeze for 1 hour before serving.

Macros: Calories 131, fat 12, fiber 1, carbs 2, sugars 0, protein 3

192. Macadamia Nuts and Coconut Bombs

Preparation time: 40 minutes
Cook time: 0 minutes
Servings: 16
Ingredients:
- ¼ cup coconut oil, melted
- ½ cup macadamia nuts, chopped
- ½ cup coconut, unsweetened and shredded
- 1 cup coconut butter, melted
- 2 tbsp. stevia
- 1 tsp vanilla extract

Preparation Instructions:
1. In a blender, combine the ingredients and pulse well.
2. Divide into silicone molds and freeze for 40 minutes before serving.

Macros: Calories 141, fat 13, fiber 2, carbs 4, sugars 0.4, protein 3

193. Ice Cream Fat Bombs

Preparation time: 4 hours
Cook time: 40 minutes
Servings: 12

Ingredients:

- ½ cup keto chocolate ice cream, soft
- 2 cups walnuts, chopped
- 10 oz. almond milk
- 1 tsp vanilla extract
- 2 tbsp. liquid stevia
- 2 cups coconut butter, melted
- 2 eggs, whisked

Preparation Instructions:

1. In a pan, combine the milk with the walnuts and vanilla, stir, bring to a simmer and cook over medium heat for 40 minutes.
2. Transfer this to a blender, add the remaining ingredients and pulse well.
3. Pour into round molds and freeze for 4 hours before serving.

Macros: Calories 166, fat 14, fiber 2, carbs 4, sugars 1, protein 3

194. Milky Fat Bombs

Preparation time: 2 hours
Cook time: 0 minutes
Servings: 12

Ingredients:

- 3 tbsp. dark chocolate, unsweetened and melted
- 1 cup almond milk
- 1 tsp vanilla powder
- ¼ cup ghee, melted
- 1 tbsp stevia
- 3 drops almond extract
- ½ cup almonds, chopped
- ½ cup coconut butter, soft

Preparation Instructions:

1. In blender, combine the ingredients and pulse well.
2. Divide into favorite molds and freeze for 2 hours before serving.

Macros: Calories 141, fat 14, fiber 2, carbs 2, sugars 4, protein 4

195. Butter Fat Bombs

Preparation time: 3 hours
Cook time: 0 minutes
Servings: 12

Ingredients:

- ½ cup cocoa butter, melted
- 2 cups almond butter
- 1 cup ghee, melted
- ½ cup coconut milk
- 1 tbsp almond extract
- ½ cup coconut, unsweetened and shredded
- ¼ tsp almond extract
- 2 tsp. chai spice

Preparation Instructions:

1. In blender, mix the ingredients and pulse well.
2. Divide into round molds, freeze for 3 hours, and serve.

Macros: Calories 151, fat 13, fiber 3, carbs 3, sugars 0, protein 3

196. Rhubarb Bombs

Preparation time: 2 hours
Cook time: 0 minutes
Servings: 10
Ingredients:
- 1 cup ghee, melted
- ½ cup coconut cream, heated
- ¼ cup almond butter, soft
- 1 cup rhubarb, minced
- ¼ tsp vanilla extract
- 2 tbsp. stevia
- Juice and zest of 1 lemon
- ½ cup coconut, shredded

Preparation Instructions:
1. In blender, combine the ingredients and pulse well.
2. Pour mixture into round molds and freeze for 2 hours before serving.

Macros: Calories 141, fat 15, fiber 1, carbs 3, sugars 3, protein 4

197. Cantaloupe Bombs

Preparation time: 1 hour
Cook time: 0 minutes
Servings: 12
Ingredients:
- 1 cup cantaloupe, peeled and blended
- ¼ cup ghee, melted
- ¼ cup coconut, unsweetened and shredded
- 2 tsp. vanilla extract
- 1 tsp gelatin mixed with 2 tsp. hot water
- 2 tbsp. swerve

Preparation Instructions:
1. In blender, combine the ingredients and pulse well.
2. Divide into round molds and freeze for 1 hour before serving.

Macros: Calories 141, fat 14, fiber 1, carbs 2, sugars 1, protein 3

198. Coconut Watermelon Fat Bombs

Preparation time: 2 hours
Cook time: 0 minutes
Servings: 12
Ingredients:
- 1 cup coconut butter, soft
- 1 cup coconut, unsweetened and shredded
- ½ cup watermelon, peeled and blended
- ½ cup ghee, melted
- 2 tbsp. stevia
- 2 tsp. vanilla extract
- 1 cup coconut cream

Preparation Instructions:
1. In a blender, combine the butter with the coconut, watermelon and the other ingredients and pulse well.
2. Divide into round molds and freeze for 2 hours before serving.

Macros: Calories 141, fat 14, fiber 3, carbs 5, sugars 1, protein 4

199. Ginger Green Bombs

Preparation time: 2 hours
Cook time: 0 minutes
Servings: 10

Ingredients:

- 1 tsp green tea powder
- 1 tsp lime zest, grated
- 1 cup almond butter, soft
- ½ cup ghee, melted
- ¼ cup coconut flakes, unsweetened
- 1 tsp vanilla extract

Preparation Instructions:

1. In a food processor, combine the ingredients and pulse well.
2. Pour into round molds and freeze for 2 hours before serving.

Macros: Calories 121, fat 11, fiber 2, carbs 4, sugars 0, protein 4

200. Cream Cheese and Cinnamon Bombs

Preparation time: 1 hour
Cook time: 0 minutes
Servings: 12

Ingredients:

- 4 oz. cream cheese, soft
- 1/3 cup ghee, melted
- 1 tbsp liquid stevia
- 1 tsp lemon zest, grated
- 1 tsp cinnamon powder

Preparation Instructions:

1. In a bowl, combine the cream cheese with the cinnamon, ghee and the rest of the ingredients and whisk well
2. Divide into ice cube trays and keep in the fridge for 1 hour before serving.

Macros: Calories 141, fat 13, fiber 1, carbs 4, sugars 0.4, protein 2

201. Sesame and Avocado Fat Bombs

Preparation time: 2 hours
Cook time: 0 minutes
Servings: 12

Ingredients:

- 1 cup coconut butter, soft
- 1 tbsp sesame seeds
- 2 tsp. vanilla extract
- 1 cup ghee, melted
- ¼ cup cocoa powder
- ½ cup avocado, peeled, pitted and mashed
- 2 tbsp. stevia

Preparation Instructions:

1. In a bowl, combine the ingredients and whisk well.
2. Divide this mixture into favorite molds and keep this in the fridge for 2 hours before serving.

Macros: Calories 131, fat 11, fiber 2, carbs 4, sugars 1, protein 3

202. Coconut Milk Fat Bombs

Preparation time: 1 hour
Cook time: 0 minutes
Servings: 10

Ingredients:

- 1 cup coconut oil, melted
- 1 cup coconut cream
- ½ cup coconut milk
- 2 tsp. vanilla extract
- 1 cup coconut flakes
- 1 tbsp gelatin mixed with 1 tbsp hot water

Preparation Instructions:

1. In a bowl, combine coconut oil with the cream, milk and other ingredients and whisk well.
2. Divide this into round molds and keep in the fridge for 1 hour before serving.

Macros: Calories 131, fat 11, fiber 2, carbs 3, sugars 1, protein 3

203. Instant Coffee Fat Bombs

Preparation time: 1 hour
Cook time: 0 minutes
Servings: 12

Ingredients:

- 1 tbsp instant coffee whisked with 2 tbsp. water
- 2 tbsp. swerve
- 3 oz. coconut butter, soft
- 1 tbsp coconut oil, melted
- 1 tbsp cocoa powder

Preparation Instructions:

1. In a blender, combine the swerve with the butter, instant coffee and the other ingredients and pulse well.
2. Pour into molds.
3. Keep in the fridge for 1 hour before serving.

Macros: Calories 62, fat 11, fiber 2, carbs 1, sugars 0.4, protein 3

204. Coconut and Almond Chocolate Bars

Preparation time: 10 minutes
Cook time: 20 minutes
Servings: 15

Ingredients

- 3.5 oz. dark chocolate, unsweetened
- 1 1/2 cups sliced almond
- 1 tbsp chia seeds
- 1 cup coconut flakes
- 1/4 tsp sea salt
- 3/4 cup coconut oil, melted
- 4 tbsp. chopped almonds

Preparation Instructions:

1. Preheat oven to 350 F.
2. Meanwhile, place a skillet over medium heat, add coconut flakes and cook for 5 minutes or until toasted. Set aside.
3. Place sliced almonds in a blender, add oil, pulse for 2 minutes until very smooth, then add coconut flakes and chia seeds and continue blending until well combined.
4. Take a 9 x 12" baking dish, line it with parchment paper, add almond mixture, spread it evenly and sprinkle with salt.
5. Place the baking dish in the freezer and let chill for 30 minutes.
6. Meanwhile, melt chocolate in microwave for 2 minutes.
7. Drizzle chocolate over frozen almond-coconut mixture, then sprinkle with chopped almonds and continue freezing for 5 minutes.
8. Then cut into squares and serve.

Macros: 227 Calories; 22.6 g Fats; 2.7 g Protein; 2.8 g Net Carb; 2.6 g Fiber

205. Cranberry Bliss Bars

Preparation time: 10 minutes
Cook time: 20 minutes
Servings: 15

Ingredients

For the Bars:

- 1 cup fresh cranberries, chopped
- 1/2 cup almond flour
- 1 tsp of baking powder
- 1/4 tsp ginger powder
- 1/4 cup coconut flour
- ¼ tsp salt
- 1/2 tsp orange extract, unsweetened
- 1/3 cup swerve sweetener
- 2 tbsp. erythritol sweetener
- 1 tsp vanilla extract, unsweetened
- 2 eggs, pastured
- 6 tbsp. softened butter, unsalted

For the Frosting:

- 1/2 cup powdered erythritol sweetener
- 1 tbsp butter, unsalted, softened
- 4 drops of lemon extract, unsweetened
- 4 oz. cream cheese, full-fat, softened

Preparation Instructions:

1. Preheat the oven to 350 F.
2. Place butter in a bowl, add swerve sweetener and whisk until creamy.
3. Whisk in eggs, salt, vanilla, and orange extract until well mixed, then whisk in remaining ingredients, berries at the end, until incorporated.
4. Grease an 8 x 8" baking dish, add the berries mixture, spread evenly, and then bake for 30 to 35 minutes or until nicely golden brown and let cool for 15 minutes.
5. Place all frosting ingredients in a bowl and beat until creamy and fluffy.
6. When the bars have baked, let them cool for 30 minutes, then top with prepared frosting and gently spread with a spatula.
7. Refrigerate the bars for 2 hours until chilled, then cut into squares and serve.

Macros:110 Calories; 10 g Fats; 2 g Protein; 2 g Net Carb; 1 g Fiber

206. Granola Bars
Preparation time: 10 minutes
Cook time: 20 minutes
Servings: 12
Ingredients
- 1/4 cup chocolate chips, stevia-sweetened
- 1 cup almonds, chopped
- 4 tbsp. erythritol sweetener
- 1 cup coconut flakes, unsweetened
- 3/4 tsp
- sea salt
- 1 cup slivered almonds
- 1 egg, pastured
- 1 tbsp coconut oil
- 2 tbsp. almond butter

Preparation Instructions:
1. Preheat the oven to 375 F.
2. Line take 3 small baking sheet with parchment papers, place coconut flakes, chopped almonds separately on each sheet and bake until toasted;
3. When done, let cool completely, leaving the oven on at 350 F.
4. Meanwhile, crack the eggs in a bowl, add sweetener and then whisk until blended.
5. Place almond butter in a heatproof bowl, add coconut oil and then heat for 30 seconds on high.
6. Add butter-oil mixture into eggs, whisk until well combined, then add cooled almonds and coconut flakes, season with salt, stir until well combined and then fold in chocolate chips until just mixed.
7. Line an 8x8" baking pan with parchment paper, add the granola mixture, spread evenly and then press firmly by using a small piece of parchment paper.
8. Bake the granola for 15 minutes, then let it cool completely at room temp and cut into twelve bars.
Macros: 194 Calories; 17.4 g Fats; 5.5 g Protein; 3.7 g Net Carb; 4.6 g Fiber

207. Chocolate Crunch Bars
Preparation time: 10 minutes
Cook time: 20 minutes
Servings: 15
Ingredients
- 1 1/2 cups of chocolate chips, stevia-sweetened
- 1 cup sliced almonds
- 1 cup cashews
- 1 cup pepitas
- 1 cup almond butter
- 1/4 cup avocado oil
- 1/2 cup swerve sweetened syrup

Preparation Instructions:
1. Place chocolate chips in a heatproof bowl, add oil, sweetened syrup and almond butter and microwave for 1 to 2 minutes on high or until melted.
2. Add remaining ingredients and stir until fully combined.
3. Line an 8x8" baking dish with parchment paper, add the prepared mixture in it and spread evenly.
4. Place the baking dish into the freezer for 2 to 3 hours or until bars are firm, then cut into pieces and serve.
Macros:179 Calories; 15 g Fats; 7 g Protein; 2 g Net Carb; 2 g Fiber

208. Peanut Butter Bars

Preparation time: 10 minutes
Cook time: 20 minutes
Servings: 6
Ingredients
For the Peanut Butter Filling:
- 5 tbsp. ground almond flour
- 1 tsp vanilla extract, unsweetened
- ½ cup peanut butter, unsweetened
- 4 tbsp. erythritol sweetener
- 4 tbsp. butter, unsalted, melted

For the Coating:
- 2.5 oz. chocolate, sugar-free

Preparation Instructions:
1. Place all filling ingredients in a bowl and stir well until smooth.
2. Take a rectangular molds silicone tray, add the prepared mixture in it and freeze for 30 minutes or until firm.
3. Then place chocolate into a heatproof bowl and microwave for 2 minutes or until chocolate has melted.
4. Pour the melted chocolate evenly on frozen bars, about 0.2-inch thick, and continue freezing the bars until solid, saving the remaining melted chocolate.
5. When bars are solid, take them out from the mold, then place them on a baking rack lined with parchment paper and pour remaining melted chocolate on the bars until covered completely.
6. Return the bars into the freezer until chilled and solid and then serve.

Macros: 315 Calories; 27.3 g Fats; 9.7 g Protein; 5 g Net Carb; 1.5 g Fiber

209. Cocoa MCT Bars

Preparation time: 10 minutes
Cook time: 20 minutes
Servings: 24
Ingredients
- 1/2 cup stevia syrup
- oz. cocoa butter
- 2 scoops MCT powder
- 1/2 cup coconut butter
- 3 tbsp. coconut oil
- 2 tsp. vanilla extract, unsweetened
- 1/3 cup heavy cream, grass-fed, full-fat

Preparation Instructions:
1. Place all the ingredients in a saucepan over low heat and cook for 5 minutes or until melted, whisking frequently.
2. Remove the pan from the heat, then take an 8x8" cake pan, line it with parchment paper, pour the mixture in it and freeze for 3 hours or until firm and chilled.
3. Cut into twenty-four pieces and serve.

Macros: 94 Calories; 9 g Fats; 0 g Protein; 0 g Net Carb; 0 g Fiber

210. Peanut Butter Protein Bars

Preparation time: 10 minutes
Cook time: 20 minutes
Servings: 8
Ingredients
For the Base Layer:
- 1 1/2 tbsp coconut flour
- 1 1/2 tbsp erythritol sweetener
- 1 tbsp whey protein powder
- 1/2 cup
- peanut butter, unsweetened

For the Top Layer:
- 1 1/2 tbsp coconut flour
- 1 tbsp whey protein powder
- 1 tbsp cocoa powder, unsweetened
- 1 1/2 tbsp powdered erythritol sweetener
- 1/2 cup peanut butter, unsweetened

Preparation Instructions:
1. Switch on the oven, set it to 350 F and let preheat.
2. Meanwhile, place all the ingredients for the base in a bowl, stir until mixed and then knead until well combined.
3. Place all the ingredients for the top layer in another bowl, stir until mixed and then knead until well combined.
4. Take a 5 by 6 inches baking dish, line it with parchment paper, add base layer mixture, spread it evenly it, then spread with top layer mixture and bake for 25 minutes or until bars are set and nicely golden brown.
5. When done, let bars cool at room temp, then cut into eight pieces and serve.

Macros: 211 Calories; 15.4 g Fats; 11.3 g Protein; 2 g Net Carb; 3.5 g Fiber

211. Chocolate Fat Bombs

Preparation time: 10 minutes
Cook time: 20 minutes
Servings: 15
Ingredients
- 2 tbsp. cashews, chopped
- 4 tbsp. coconut flour
- 2 tbsp. almonds, chopped
- ½ cup cocoa powder, unsweetened
- 1 cup almond butter, melted
- 1 cup melted coconut oil

Preparation Instructions:
1. Take a small saucepan, place it over medium heat, add coconut oil and butter and heat for 3 minutes or more until melted, stirring frequently.
2. Pour mixture into a freezer ready bowl, add cocoa and coconut flour and then stir well.
3. Place the bowl into the freezer and let chill for 1 hour or until the mixture is solid.
4. Then shape the mixture into balls by scooping out about ½ tbsp at a time and cover the balls into cashews and almonds until well coated.
5. Prepare and coat all the balls in the same manner, then place them on a cool plate and refrigerate for 15 minutes until chilled.
6. Serve straight away.

Macros: 174 Calories; 17 g Fats; 3 g Protein; 2 g Net Carb; 2 g Fiber

212. Peanut Butter Fat Bombs

Preparation time: 10 minutes
Cook time: 20 minutes
Servings: 15
Ingredients
- 1/4 cup peanut butter, full-fat, unsweetened, softened
- 4 oz. cream cheese, full-fat, softened
- 2 tbsp. swerve sweetener

Preparation Instructions:
1. Place softened peanut butter in a bowl, add the swerve sweetener and stir until well mixed.
2. Place cream cheese in a heatproof bowl, microwave for 5 seconds at high heat setting unit very soft, then add it into peanut butter mixture and stir well until very smooth.
3. Take a fourteen round molds silicone tray, evenly divide the batter into the molds and chill in the freezer for 2 hours or until solid.
4. Serve straight away.

Macros: 50 Calories; 5 g Fats; 2 g Protein; 0.5 g Net Carb; 0.5 g Fiber

213. Red Velvet Fat Bombs

Preparation time: 10 minutes
Cook time: 20 minutes
Servings: 15
Ingredients
- 3.5 oz. dark chocolate, stevia-sweetened
- 3 tbsp. liquid stevia
- 3.5 oz. butter, unsalted, softened
- 4 drops red food coloring
- 1 tsp vanilla extract, unsweetened
- 4.4 oz. cream cheese, full-fat, softened
- 1/3 cup whipped heavy cream, grass-fed, full-fat

Preparation Instructions:
1. Place chocolate in a heatproof bowl and microwave for 1 to 2 minutes or until it melts.
2. Place remaining ingredients in another bowl, except for heavy cream, whisk until well combined and then whisk in melted chocolate at low speed until mixed.
3. Pour mixture into a piping bag, then pipe the mixture onto a baking tray lined with parchment paper in 24 sections and refrigerate for 40 minutes.
4. Top fat bombs with heavy cream, continue refrigerating until firm and then serve.

Macros: 59 Calories; 6 g Fats; 0 g Protein; 0 g Net Carb; 0 g Fiber

214. Pecan Fat Bombs

Preparation time: 10 minutes
Cook time: 20 minutes
Servings: 9
Ingredients
- 9 pecans
- 1 scoop collagen powder, grass-fed, vanilla flavored
- 2 tbsp. stevia syrup
- 4 oz. butter, unsalted
- 2 oz. pecan butter

Preparation Instructions:
1. Take a small saucepan, place all the ingredients in it, except for pecan, then place the saucepan over low heat and cook for 5 minutes or until heated through, frequently whisking until well combined.
2. Then remove the saucepan from heat, let it cool for 5 minutes and then pour the mixture into a heatproof dish, lined with parchment paper.
3. Sprinkle with pecan nuts, press them slightly into the mixture and freeze for 1 to 2 hours or until firm.
4. Cut the frozen mix into nine pieces and serve.

Macros: 147 Calories; 15 g Fats; 3 g Protein; 0 g Net Carb; 1 g Fiber

215. Lemon Fat Bombs

Preparation time: 10 minutes
Cook time: 20 minutes
Servings: 15

Ingredients

- 1 lemon, zested and juiced
- 2 tbsp. butter, unsalted
- 1 tbsp erythritol sweetener
- 2 tbsp. coconut butter
- 2 tbsp. coconut oil

Preparation Instructions:

1. Place all the ingredients in a saucepan over low heat and cook for 5 minutes or until melted, whisking frequently.
2. Remove from heat and pour the mixture evenly into a rectangular molds silicone tray and freeze for 1 hour or until set and chilled.

Macros: 40 Calories; 4 g Fats; 1 g Protein; 0.5 g Net Carb; 0.5 g Fiber

CAKES

216. Flourless Chocolate Cake

Preparation time: 10 minutes
Cook time: 45 minutes
Servings: 6

Ingredients:
- ½ Cup of stevia
- 12 oz. of unsweetened baking chocolate
- 2/3 Cup of ghee
- 1/3 Cup of warm water
- ¼ tsp of salt
- 4 eggs
- 2 Cups of boiling water

Preparation Instructions:
1. Line the bottom of a 9-inch springform pan with parchment paper.
2. Heat the water in a small pot; then add the salt and the stevia over the water until wait until the mixture becomes completely dissolved.
3. Melt baking chocolate into a double boiler or microwave it for 30 seconds.
4. Mix the melted chocolate and butter in a large bowl with an electric mixer.
5. Beat in hot mixture; then crack in the egg and whisk after adding each of the eggs.
6. Pour mixture into spring form tray.
7. Wrap the spring form tray with foil.
8. Place the spring form tray in a large cake tray and add boiling water to the outside; make sure the depth doesn't exceed 1 inch.
9. Bake the cake in the water bath for 45 minutes at 350 F.
10. Remove the tray from the boiling water and transfer to a wire to cool.
11. Let the cake chill overnight in the refrigerator.

Macros: Calories: 295, Fat: 26g, Carbohydrates: 6g, Fiber: 4g, Protein: 8g

217. Raspberry Cake with White Chocolate Sauce

Preparation time: 15 minutes
Cook time: 60 minutes
Servings: 5-6

Ingredients:

- 5 oz. of melted cacao butter
- 2 oz. of grass-fed ghee
- ½ Cup of coconut cream
- 1 Cup of green banana flour
- 3 tsp. of pure vanilla
- 4 large eggs
- ½ Cup of Lakanto Monk Fruit
- 1 tsp of baking powder
- 2 tsp. of apple cider vinegar
- 2 Cup of raspberries

For the white chocolate sauce:

- 3 ½ oz. of cacao butter
- ½ Cup of coconut cream
- 2 tsp. of pure vanilla extract
- 1 Pinch of salt

Preparation Instructions:

1. Preheat oven to 280 F.
2. Combine the green banana flour with pure vanilla extract, baking powder, coconut cream, eggs, cider vinegar and the monk fruit and mix well.
3. Set the raspberries aside and line a cake loaf tin with parchment paper .
4. Pour batter into the baking tray and scatter the raspberries over the top of the cake.
5. Place the tray in the oven and bake it for 60 minutes

for sauce:

1. Combine the cacao cream, vanilla extract, cacao butter and salt in a saucepan over low heat.
2. Mix all ingredients with a fork to make sure the cacao butter mixes well with the cream.
3. Remove from the heat.
4. Drizzle with the chocolate sauce.
5. Scatter the cake with more raspberries.

Macros: Calories: 323, Fat: 31.5g, Carbohydrates: 9.9g, Fiber: 4g, Protein: 5g

218. Keto Lava Cake

Preparation time: 10 minutes
Cook time: 10 minutes
Servings: 2

Ingredients:

- 2 oz of dark chocolate
- 1 tbsp of super-fine almond flour
- 2 oz of unsalted almond butter
- 2 large eggs

Preparation Instructions:

1. Heat oven to 350 F.
2. Grease 2 heatproof ramekins.
3. Melt the chocolate and almond butter and stir very well.
4. Beat the eggs well with a mixer.
5. Add the eggs to the chocolate and butter mixture and mix well with almond flour and swerve; then stir.
6. Pour the dough into 2 ramekins. Bake for about 9 to 10 minutes.
7. Serve with pomegranate seeds.

Macros: Calories: 459, Fat: 39g, Carbohydrates: 3.5g, Fiber: 0.8g, Protein: 11.7g

219. Keto Cheesecake

Preparation time: 4 hours
Cook time: 15 minutes
Servings: 6

Ingredients:

For the Almond Flour Crust:
- 2 Cups of Blanched almond flour
- 1/3 Cup of almond Butter
- 3 tbsp. of Erythritol (powdered or granular)
- 1 tsp of Vanilla extract

For the Keto Cheesecake Filling:
- 32 oz of softened Cream cheese
- 1 and ¼ cups of powdered erythritol
- 3 large eggs
- 1 tbsp of Lemon juice
- 1 tsp of Vanilla extract

Preparation Instructions:
1. Preheat oven to 350 F.
2. Grease a 9" springform pan with cooking spray or line with parchment paper.
3. Mix melted butter, almond flour, vanilla extract and erythritol in a large bowl.
4. The dough will get will be a bit crumbly; press it into the bottom of prepared tray.
5. Bake for 12 minutes; then let cool for 10 minutes.
6. In the meantime, beat the softened cream cheese and powdered sweetener at a low speed until smooth.
7. Add eggs one at a time and beat them in at a low to medium speed until it becomes fluffy.
8. Add in lemon juice and vanilla extract and mix at a low to medium speed.
9. Pour filling into pan on top of the crust.
10. Bake for 45 to 50 minutes.
11. Remove the baked cheesecake from oven and run a knife around its edge.
12. Let the cake cool for 4 hours in the refrigerator.

Macros: Calories: 325, Fat: 29g, Carbohydrates: 6g, Fiber: 1g, Protein: 7g

220. Cake with Whipped Cream Icing

Preparation time: 20 minutes
Cook time: 25 minutes
Servings: 7

Ingredients:
- ¾ Cup Coconut flour
- ¾ Cup of Swerve Sweetener
- ½ Cup of Cocoa powder
- 2 tsp. of baking powder
- 6 large eggs
- 2/3 Cup of Heavy Whipping Cream
- ½ Cup of Melted almond Butter

For the whipped Cream Icing:
- 1 Cup of Heavy Whipping Cream
- ¼ Cup of Swerve Sweetener
- 1 tsp of Vanilla extract
- 1/3 Cup of Sifted Cocoa Powder

Preparation Instructions:
1. Preheat oven to 350 F.
2. Grease an 8x8" cake tray with cooking spray.
3. Add the coconut flour, Swerve; cocoa powder, baking powder, eggs, and melted butter; combine well.
4. Pour batter into the cake tray and bake for 25 minutes.
5. For the Icing
6. Whip the cream until it becomes fluffy; then add in the Swerve, vanilla and cocoa powder. Mix well.
7. Frost baked cake with the icing

Macros: Calories: 357, Fat: 33g, Carbohydrates: 11g, Fiber: 2g, Protein: 8g

221. Walnut Fruitcake

Preparation time: 15 minutes
Cook time: 20 minutes
Servings: 6

Ingredients:
- 1/2 Cup of almond butter (softened)
- ¼ Cup of so Nourished granulated erythritol
- 1 tbsp of ground cinnamon
- ½ tsp of ground nutmeg
- ¼ tsp of ground cloves
- 4 large pastured eggs
- 1 tsp of vanilla extract
- ½ tsp of almond extract
- 2 Cups of almond flour
- ½ Cup of chopped walnuts
- ¼ Cup of dried of unsweetened cranberries
- ¼ Cup of seedless raisins

Preparation Instructions:
1. Preheat oven to 350 F and grease an 8-inch round baking tin with coconut oil.
2. Beat the granulated erythritol on a high speed until it becomes fluffy.
3. Add the cinnamon, nutmeg, and cloves; blend until smooth.
4. Add eggs one at a time, plus the almond extract and the vanilla.
5. Whisk in almond flour until it forms a smooth batter then fold in the nuts and fruit.
6. Spread mixture into prepared baking pan and bake for 20 minutes.
7. Dust the cake with the powdered erythritol.

Macros: Calories: 250, Fat: 11g, Carbohydrates: 12g, Fiber: 2g, Protein: 7g

222. Ginger Cake

Preparation time: 15 minutes
Cook time: 20 minutes
Servings: 9

Ingredients:
- ½ tbsp of unsalted almond butter to grease the pan
- 4 large eggs
- ¼ Cup coconut milk
- 2 tbsp. of unsalted almond butter
- 1 and ½ tsp. of stevia
- 1 tbsp of ground cinnamon
- 1 tbsp of natural unsweetened cocoa powder
- 1 tbsp of fresh ground ginger
- ½ tsp of kosher salt
- 1 and ½ cups of blanched almond flour
- ½ tsp of baking soda

Preparation Instructions:
1. Preheat oven to 325 F.
2. Grease a 8x8" glass baking tray.
3. In a large bowl, whisk the coconut milk, eggs, melted almond butter, stevia, cinnamon, cocoa powder, ginger and salt.
4. Whisk in the almond flour and baking soda and mix well.
5. Pour the batter into the pan and bake for 20 to 25 minutes.

Macros: Calories: 175, Fat: 15g, Carbohydrates: 5g, Fiber: 1.9g, Protein: 5g

223. Keto Orange Cake

Preparation time: 10 minutes
Cook time: 50 minutes
Servings: 8
Ingredients:
- 2 ½ cups of almond flour
- 2 washed oranges
- 5 large separated eggs
- 1 tsp of baking powder
- 2 tsp. of orange extract
- 1 tsp of vanilla bean powder
- 6 cardamom seeds, crushed
- 16 drops of liquid stevia
- 1 handful of flaked almonds to decorate

Preparation Instructions:
1. Preheat oven to 350 F.
2. Line a rectangular bread baking tray with parchment paper.
3. Place the oranges into a pan filled with cold water and cover it with a lid. Bring the saucepan to a boil, then let simmer for about 1 hour and make sure the oranges are totally submerged.
4. Cut the oranges into halves, remove seeds, and drain the water.
5. Cool oranges and puree with a blender or a food processor.
6. Separate the eggs; whisk the egg whites until stiff peaks form.
7. Add all ingredients except for the egg whites to the orange mixture, then add in the egg whites; mix.
8. Pour batter into the cake tin and sprinkle with flaked almonds right on top.
9. Bake for about 50 minutes.

Macros: Calories: 164, Fat: 12g, Carbohydrates: 7.1, Fiber: 2.7g, Protein: 10.9g

224. Lemon Cake

Preparation time: 20 minutes
Cook time: 20 minutes
Servings: 9
Ingredients:
- 2 medium lemons
- 4 large eggs
- 2 tbsp. of almond butter
- 2 tbsp. of avocado oil
- 1/3 cup of coconut flour
- 4-5 tbsp. of honey (or another sweetener of choice)
- ½ tbsp of baking soda

Preparation Instructions:
1. Preheat oven to 350 F.
2. Crack the eggs in a large bowl and set two egg whites aside.
3. Whisk 2 whites of eggs with the egg yolks, honey, oil, almond butter, the lemon zest and juice and mix well.
4. Combine the baking soda with the coconut flour and gradually add the dry mixture to the wet ingredients and keep whisking for a couple of minutes.
5. Beat the two eggs with a hand mixer and beat the egg into foam.
6. Add the white egg foam gradually.
7. Transfer batter to tray lined with parchment paper.
8. Bake for 20 to 22 minutes.

Macros: Calories: 164, Fat: 12g, Carbohydrates: 7.1, Fiber: 2.7g, Protein: 10.9g

225. Cinnamon Cake

Preparation time: 15 minutes
Cook time: 35 minutes
Servings: 8

Ingredients

For the Filling:
- 3 tbsp. of Swerve Sweetener
- 2 tsp. of ground cinnamon

For the Cake:
- 3 Cups of almond flour
- ¾ Cup of Swerve Sweetener
- ¼ Cup of unflavored whey protein powder
- 2 tsp of baking powder
- ½ tsp of salt
- 3 large pastured eggs
- ½ Cup of melted coconut oil
- ½ tsp of vanilla extract
- ½ Cup of almond milk
- 1 tbsp of melted coconut oil

For the Frosting:
- 3 tbsp. of softened cream cheese
- 2 tbsp. of powdered Swerve Sweetener
- 1 tbsp of coconut heavy whipping cream
- ½ tsp of vanilla extract

Preparation Instructions:

1. Preheat oven to 325 F and grease a 8x8" baking tray.
2. For the filling, mix the Swerve and cinnamon in a mixing bowl; set it aside.
3. For the cake, whisk the almond flour, sweeteners, protein powder, baking powder, and salt in a mixing bowl.
4. Add in the eggs, the melted coconut oil and vanilla extract and mix well.
5. Add in the almond milk and keep stirring until ingredients are well combined.
6. Spread about half of the batter in the prepared pan; then sprinkle with about two thirds of the filling mixture.
7. Spread the remaining mixture of the batter over the filling and smooth it with a spatula.
8. Bake for 35 minutes.
9. Brush with the melted coconut oil and sprinkle with the remaining cinnamon filling.
10. Prepare the frosting by beating the cream cheese, powdered erythritol, cream and vanilla extract in a mixing bowl until smooth.
11. Drizzle frosting over cooled cake.

Macros: Calories: 222, Fat: 19.2g, Carbohydrates: 5.4g, Fiber: 1.5g, Protein: 7.3g

226. Macadamia Nuts Cake

Preparation time: 10 minutes
Cook time: 35 minutes
Servings: 4

Ingredients:
- 1 cup macadamia nuts, chopped
- 2 eggs, whisked
- ½ cup coconut cream
- 1 cup coconut milk
- 1 and ½ cups coconut flour
- ½ tsp cinnamon powder
- ½ tsp of baking powder
- ½ tsp of baking soda

Preparation Instructions:
1. In a bowl, combine the nuts with the eggs, cream, milk and other ingredients, and whisk well.
2. Pour this into a cake pan lined with parchment paper, spread, and bake at 365 F for 35 minutes.
3. Cool the cake down, slice and serve.

Macros: Calories 220, fat 3, fiber 5, carbs 16, protein 4

227. Stevia and Avocado Cake

Preparation time: 10 minutes
Cook time: 40 minutes
Servings: 8

Ingredients:
- 2 cups coconut flour
- 1 cup coconut milk
- ½ cup coconut cream
- 1 avocado, peeled, pitted and mashed
- 1 cup almond butter
- 1 tsp vanilla extract
- 4 tbsp. stevia
- 2 tsp. baking powder

Preparation Instructions:
1. In a bowl, mix the coconut flour with the milk, cream and the other ingredients, whisk and pour into a cake pan lined with parchment paper.
2. Bake at 350 F for 40 minutes, cool down, slice and serve.

Macros: Calories 200, fat 10, fiber 5, carbs 17, protein 4

228. Mint and Coconut Cake

Preparation time: 3 hours and 10 minutes
Cook time: 0 minutes
Servings: 6
Ingredients:
- ¼ cup coconut oil, melted
- 1 cup flaxseed
- ¼ cup stevia

For the first layer:
- 1 cup almond flour
- ½ cup water
- 1 tbsp lime juice
- 1/6 cup mint, chopped
- 2 tbsp. stevia
- 1 tbsp coconut oil, melted
- 2 tbsp. chia seeds

For the second layer:
- 1 cup coconut flakes, unsweetened
- 1 tbsp lemon juice
- ½ cup water
- 1 tbsp coconut oil, melted
- 3 tbsp. stevia
- 1 tsp vanilla extract
- 2 tbsp. chia seeds

Preparation Instructions:
1. In a blender, mix the coconut oil with the flaxseed and ¼ cup stevia; pulse well. Transfer into a cake pan, spread on the bottom and refrigerate.
2. Blend the almond flour with ½ cup water and the ingredients for the first layer, pulse well and transfer to a bowl.
3. Clean the blender, add the coconut flakes, lemon juice and the other ingredients for the second layer.
4. Take cake crust out of the fridge, spread the first and the second layer, and cook the cake for 3 hours before serving.

Macros: Calories 370, fat 8, fiber 8, carbs 20, protein 3

229. Tangerine Cake

Preparation time: 10 minutes
Cook time: 30 minutes
Servings: 4
Ingredients:
- 2 cups coconut flour
- ¼ cup avocado oil
- ½ cup coconut milk
- 1 tsp almond extract
- 2 tangerines, peeled and chopped
- 1 tsp of baking powder
- ½ cup coconut cream
- ½ tsp vanilla extract
- Juice and zest of 1 lime

Preparation Instructions:
1. In a bowl, combine the ingredients, whisk well, pour into a greased cake pan
2. Bake at 375 F for 30 minutes, cooled down, slice and serve.

Macros: Calories 190, fat 5, fiber 7, carbs 20, protein 6

230. Date and Vanilla Cake

Preparation time: 10 minutes
Cook time: 25 minutes
Servings: 4

Ingredients:

- 1 cup almond flour
- 1 cup almond milk
- ½ cup dates
- ½ cup almonds, chopped
- 2 tbsp. stevia
- 1 tsp vanilla extract
- ½ cup coconut oil, melted
- 1 tsp of baking powder
- 1 tsp of baking soda
- ¼ tsp cinnamon powder
- Juice of 1 lemon

Preparation Instructions:

1. In a blender, mix the almond flour with the milk, dates and the other ingredients and pulse well.
2. Transfer to a cake pan lined with parchment paper, and bake at 370 F for 25 minutes.

Macros: Calories 255, fat 5, fiber 8, carbs 20, protein 4

231. Ginger Cake

Preparation time: 10 minutes
Cook time: 35 minutes
Servings: 4

Ingredients:

- 3 eggs, whisked
- 1 cup almond flour
- 1 cup almond milk
- 1 tsp of baking powder
- 2 tbsp. stevia
- 2 tsp. ginger, grated
- 1 tsp of baking soda
- 1 tsp cinnamon powder
- 1/3 cup avocado oil, soft

Preparation Instructions:

1. In a bowl, combine the ingredients and whisk well.
2. Pour into a cake pan lined with parchment paper, bake at 350 F for 35 minutes, cool it down, slice and serve.

Macros: Calories 271, fat 8, fiber 8, carbs 18, protein 8

232. Cocoa and Macadamia Cake

Preparation time: 10 minutes
Cook time: 30 minutes
Servings: 6
Ingredients:
- 1 cup almond flour
- 1 cup almond milk
- 2 tbsp. cocoa powder
- 1 cup coconut cream
- ½ tsp cinnamon powder
- 2 tbsp. macadamia nuts
- 1 tsp of baking powder
- 1 tbsp cocoa nibs
- 1 ½ tbsp coconut oil, melted

Preparation Instructions:
1. In a blender, mix the ingredients, whisk well and pour into a cake pan lined with parchment paper.
2. Bake the cake at 360 F for 30 minutes, cooled down, slice and serve.

Macros: Calories 160, fat 2, fiber 6, carbs 22, protein 1

233. Berry and Avocado Cake

Preparation time: 5 hours and 10 minutes
Cook time: 0 minutes
Servings: 6
Ingredients:
For the crust:
- ½ cup dates, pitted
- 1 tbsp water
- ½ tsp vanilla extract
- ½ cup walnuts, chopped

For the cake:
- 2 cups walnuts, chopped
- ½ cup avocado, peeled, pitted and mashed
- 1 cup blueberries
- 3 tbsp. stevia
- 1 tbsp avocado oil

Preparation Instructions:
1. In blender, combine the dates with water, vanilla and ½ cup walnuts, pulse well. Flatten into a greased cake pan.
2. Clean blender, add 2 cups walnuts, avocado and other cake ingredients, pulse well, spread over the cake crust, refrigerate for 5 hours, cut and serve.

Macros: Calories 230, fat 0.5, fiber 6, carbs 12, protein 4

234. Tomato Cake

Preparation time: 10 minutes
Cook time: 30 minutes
Servings: 6
Ingredients:
- 2 cups almond flour
- 1 tsp of baking powder
- 1 tsp cinnamon powder
- 1 tsp of baking soda
- ¾ cup stevia
- 1 cup tomatoes, chopped
- ½ cup ghee, melted

Preparation Instructions:
In a blender, combine the ingredients, pulse well, pour into a cake pan lined with parchment paper, bake at 375 F for 30 minutes, cooled down, slice and serve.

Macros: Calories 171, fat 3, fiber 7, carbs 18, protein 5

235. Beet Cake

Preparation time: 10 minutes
Cook time: 30 minutes
Servings: 6
Ingredients:
- 1 cup beets, peeled and grated
- 1 cup coconut flour
- 1 cup coconut cream
- ½ tsp gelatin powder
- ½ tsp of baking powder
- 2 eggs, whisked
- ½ cup coconut milk
- 3 tbsp. stevia
- 1/3 cup avocado oil
- ½ tsp vanilla extract

Preparation Instructions:
In a blender, combine the ingredients, pulse well, pour into a cake pan lined with parchment paper, bake at 350 F and bake for 30 minutes, cooled down, slice and serve.
Macros: Calories 148, fat 6, fiber 8, crabs 12, protein 5

236. Simple Coconut Cake

Preparation time: 10 minutes
Cook time: 30 minutes
Servings: 10
Ingredients:
- 2 cups coconut flour
- 1 cup coconut flakes, unsweetened
- 1 cup coconut milk
- 1 cup coconut cream
- 2 eggs, whisked
- ½ tsp cinnamon powder
- ½ tsp of baking soda
- 1 tsp of baking powder
- ½ cup coconut oil
- ¼ tsp nutmeg, ground
- 1 tsp vanilla extract

Preparation Instructions:
1. In blender, combine the ingredients and pulse well.
2. Pour into a cake pan lined with parchment paper, bake at 350 F for 30 minutes, cooled down, slice and serve.
Macros: Calories 214, fat 11, fiber 6, carbs 17, protein 6

237. Vanilla Tomato Cake

Preparation time: 10 minutes
Cook time: 30 minutes
Servings: 10
Ingredients:
- ¾ cup almond flour
- ½ cup stevia
- 1 cup almond milk
- 2 eggs, whisked
- ½ tsp of baking soda
- ½ tsp vanilla extract
- ½ tsp of baking powder
- ¼ cup tomatoes puree

Preparation Instructions:
1.   In a bowl, combine stevia with the flour, milk and other ingredients, whisk well and pour into a cake pan lined with parchment paper.
2.   Bake at 375 F for 30 minutes, cooled down, slice and serve.
Macros: Calories 167, fat 10, fiber 6, carbs 15, protein 4

238. Matcha Chocolate Cake

Preparation time: 10 minutes
Cook time: 30 minutes
Servings: 6
Ingredients:
- 1 cup almond flour
- 1 tsp matcha powder
- 1 cup dark chocolate, unsweetened and melted
- 1 cup almond milk
- ½ tsp of baking powder
- 1 tsp gelatin powder
- ½ cup soft coconut butter
- 3 tbsp. stevia
- 1 tsp coconut oil, melted

Preparation Instructions:
1.   In a bowl, combine the flour with the chocolate, matcha powder and the other ingredients, whisk and pour into a cake pan lined with parchment paper.
2.   Bake at 370 F for 30 minutes, cooled down, slice and serve.
Macros: Calories 160, fat 2, fiber 7, carbs 14, protein 3

239. Almond, Flaxseed and Coconut Cake

Preparation time: 10 minutes
Cook time: 30 minutes
Servings: 6
Ingredients:
- 2 cups coconut flour
- 1 cup coconut milk
- ½ cup coconut cream
- ½ cup almonds, chopped
- 2 tbsp. flaxseed
- ½ tsp vanilla extract
- 2 eggs, whisked
- 1 and ½ tsp of baking powder
- 1 tsp of baking soda
- 1 tsp cinnamon powder
- ¼ cup avocado oil

Preparation Instructions:
1.   In a bowl, combine the ingredients, whisk well and pour into a cake pan lined with parchment paper.
2.   Bake at 370 F for 30 minutes, cooled down, slice and serve.
Macros: Calories 168, fat 7, fiber 6, carbs 23, protein 6

240. Cocoa, Chia and Avocado Cake

Preparation time: 10 minutes
Cook time: 30 minutes
Servings: 8
Ingredients:
- 2 cups coconut flour
- 1 cup almond milk
- 1 tbsp chia seeds
- 1 avocado, peeled, pitted and mashed
- 2 tbsp. cocoa powder
- 1 tsp of baking powder
- 3 tbsp. avocado oil
- 2 eggs, whisked
- 3 tbsp. stevia

Preparation Instructions:
1. In a bowl, mix the ingredients, whisk well and pour into a cake pan lined with parchment paper.
2. Bake at 360 F for 30 minutes, cooled down, slice and serve.

Macros: Calories 79, fat 3, fiber 2, carbs 9, protein 3

241. Lemon Raspberry and Coconut Cake

Preparation time: 10 minutes
Cook time: 30 minutes
Servings: 8
Ingredients:
- 1 cup almond flour
- ½ cup almond butter, soft
- 1 cup almond milk
- ½ cup coconut flakes, unsweetened
- Juice of 1 lemon
- 1 cup raspberries
- 1 tsp of baking powder
- 2 eggs, whisked
- 1 tsp vanilla extract

Preparation Instructions:
1. In a bowl, mix the ingredients, whisk and pour into a cake pan lined with parchment paper.
2. Bake at 375 F for 30 minutes, cooled down, slice and serve.

Macros: Calories 109, fat 1.6, fiber 3, carbs 15, protein 5

242. Blackberry and Mint Cake

Preparation time: 10 minutes
Cook time: 30 minutes
Servings: 6
Ingredients:
- 1 cup almond flour
- ¼ tsp of baking powder
- 1 tbsp stevia
- 1 cup blackberries
- 1 tbsp mint, dried
- 1/3 cup almond milk
- ½ cup coconut cream
- ½ tsp lemon zest, grated
- ¼ tsp vanilla extract

Preparation Instructions:
1. In a bowl, combine the almond flour with the baking powder, stevia, berries and the other ingredients, and whisk well.
2. Pour this into a cake pan lined with parchment paper, cook at 375 F for 30 minutes, cooled down, slice and serve.

Macros: Calories 200, fat 4, fiber 4, carbs 10, protein 4

243. Date, Cantaloupe and Watermelon Cake

Preparation time: 10 minutes
Cook time: 25 minutes
Servings: 4
Ingredients:
- ½ cup dates, chopped
- ½ cup cantaloupe, peeled and chopped
- ½ cup watermelon, peeled and chopped
- 1 cup coconut cream
- 1 tsp gelatin powder
- 1 cup almond flour
- 1 tsp of baking powder
- 1 tsp vanilla extract

Preparation Instructions:
1. In a blender, combine the ingredients, pulse well and transfer to a cake pan lined with parchment paper.
2. Bake the cake at 370 F for 25 minutes, cool down slice and serve.

Macros: Calories 120, fat 13, fiber 4, carbs 12, protein 4

CPSIA information can be obtained
at www.ICGtesting.com
Printed in the USA
LVHW022149111220
673921LV00010B/499

9 781649 844402